BOOK ONE

Of the Soul Journey Trilogy

THE SHATTERING

(The Shattering · The Turning · The Rising)

When God Went Silent:

Grief, Ruin, and Finding a Divine Who Wanted Me

LEA RILEY

Sacred Threads
PUBLISHING

For permission requests, write to the publisher at:
Sacred Threads Publishing
Info@TheLeaRiley.com
TheLeaRiley.com

Printed in the United States of America
First Edition
ISBN: 979-8-9995558-0-9

This book is a work of creative nonfiction. Some names and
identifying details have been changed to protect the privacy of
individuals.

For my late husband, Randy –

whose death broke me open
and yet opened the way to everything that followed

For my husband now, David –

who walks beside me and anchors me,
gave me space to grieve,
and stood steady while I wrote my way through the dark.

TABLE OF CONTENTS

PART ONE: Cracks in the Foundation

Introduction

This is not a book I ever imagined writing. It was born from the wreckage of a life I never imagined surviving. Part confession, part offering, part quiet rebellion.

It was not written simply to tell the story of what happened — but to lay bare what it meant and how it shaped me to who I am today.

When my husband died, my world did not just fracture — it detonated. In an instant, everything I had built my life upon — love, marriage, faith, identity, family, dreams — was reduced to ash. Snuffed out like a candle flame extinguished. And yet, when the dust began to settle, I realized the real work had only begun.

This is a book about walking through grief, yes — but it is also a book about walking through fire. About realizing that loss doesn't take the people we love; it burns away the illusions, the false identities, the old stories we've been told about who we are, what we're worth, and what we're allowed to believe.

In many ways, this book is a map — but it is not a map with clear roads or tidy directions. It is the kind of map you trace with your fingertips in the dark, feeling for shape, for meaning, for the next breath when the path forward disappears.

Part One: Cracks in the Foundation

This section traces the raw, unfiltered aftermath of profound loss — the death of my husband, the unraveling of the life we had built, and the emotional and financial collapse that followed.

It covers the shock, the grief, the "what ifs" that haunted my mind, the painful logistics of funerals and financial collapse, and the quiet, sleepless hours when the absence felt unbearable.

It also explores the explosive rupture in my faith — the disillusionment with the religious institutions I once trusted, and the slow, painful awakening to the reality that grief does not follow a neat timeline.

Part One is the story of survival — moment by moment, hour by hour, second by second — while questioning everything I thought I knew about life, love, God, and myself.

Part Two: The Unraveling and the Becoming

This section moves into the deeper inner journey — the unraveling of old shadows, the facing of long-buried patterns, and the courageous rebuilding of my spiritual and emotional self.

It explores the shift from religious indoctrination to personal, soul-led spirituality, the healing that comes from embracing both grief and joy, and the fierce reclamation of my own voice, needs, and power.

Here, I reflect on the parts of myself I'm still working to integrate — the righteous anger, the fear of loss, the longing to be fully seen and loved — and how spiritual work has molded me into the woman I am becoming.

Part Two is not the end of the story, but the beginning of a new chapter: one where I stand rooted in my own truth, no longer surviving for others, but living fully, fiercely, and unapologetically for myself.

Together, these chapters trace the arc from devastation to transformation, from silence to voice, from loss to a living, breathing faith that no longer comes from fear, but from freedom.

This is a book about healing — not in the polished, social-media sense, but in the raw, bloodied, holy sense. The kind of healing that asks you to confront not just your pain, but your survival mechanisms, your spiritual disillusionment, your deepest shadows.

It is about remembering — not the life I lost, but the woman I had once been, the woman I buried under years of pleasing, enduring, performing. This is a book about reclaiming that woman — and, more importantly, reclaiming the woman I was always meant to become.

It is about helping others — not by offering neat answers or prescriptions, but by offering presence.

I offer you my story not because I have figured it all out, but because I have walked through enough darkness to know you don't have to walk through yours alone.

I offer you my journey because I know what it is to sit in the ruins of a life and wonder if anything sacred could possibly grow again. And I am here to tell you:

It can.

It does.

You are not beyond its reach.

Finally, this book is a teaching. Not the teaching of an old, punishing God, but of a new kind of Creator — one who lives not only in the heavens, but in you. This is a book about stepping beyond religious indoctrination, beyond shame, beyond fear, and realizing:

You carry divine potential.

You carry Creator energy.

You are not here merely to endure life — you are here to shape it, co-create with it, rise from it, and awaken into the truth that you are so much more than you were ever taught to believe.

This story goes beyond me. It is a mirror, an offering, a light for anyone walking their own path of loss and becoming. Chapter by chapter, you are invited to walk this path with me — through grief, through reclamation, through spiritual awakening, into a life shaped not by survival, but by soul.

You are not alone.

You have never been alone.

And everything you need to step forward is already inside you — waiting.

Let's begin.

Chapter One:
The Night That Never Ended

*"One night tore the ground out from under me —
and I learned you can scream and still not wake from the
nightmare."*

When God Went Silent

The Shattering

I will never forget the sound my own body made that night. The scream that ripped out of me came from somewhere beyond language — part pain, part disbelief, part animal. It was a raw, primal sound, the kind of scream you never want to hear from yourself or anyone else. It's a sound burned into my ears, my memory, and my soul.

It was March 2013 when my world didn't split in half — it *exploded*. Like a nuclear bomb detonating at the center of my life, leaving nothing untouched.

My husband seemed fine that morning. Gone by that night. No warning. No illness. No slow goodbye. A sudden, brutal absence. A flame blown out without explanation.

I tried to reach him all day, but there was no answer. It was unlike him not to return my calls. As the hours passed, my mind began drifting into those *what if* scenarios — that creeping sense that something wasn't right. After work, I decided to stop by our other property.

As I rounded the corner, I saw his truck parked in the driveway. A sigh of relief — he was here, at least.

I walked up to the door and tried to open it — locked. I banged on it, again and again, thinking maybe he was asleep. No answer.

That's when the pit started forming in my stomach.

Something didn't feel right. I called his dad to see if he'd talked to him that day. No, he hadn't. His dad told me not to worry — *Maybe he had someone help him pick up the motorcycle from the repair shop,* he suggested. I hung up, trying to shake the unease, but it stayed with me. A constant nagging.

I left, having to get to my second job, but I couldn't settle. I kept calling. No answer. I kept going over the scene at the camper. Over and over. Something is wrong.

Then it hit me.

Wait.

It wasn't the bottom lock I'd seen locked earlier — it was the deadbolt. The top lock. You can only lock that deadbolt from the inside. That didn't make sense. Panic struck me like a lightening bolt.

My heart began to race. My mind ran through a dozen possible explanations, none of them good.

I left work, drove back, heart pounding. When I arrived, the camper was dark. His truck was still parked outside. The deadbolt was still locked. I looked around and found an unlocked window. *Why is this unlocked?* I wondered. He never left the windows unlocked.

I set a folding chair under the window and carefully climbed onto it, balancing on the back of the chair as I crawled through at 11:00 p.m., my heart pounded so loud it echoed in my ears.

As soon as I was inside, I knew. I saw the blanket on the floor with something wrapped in it. I walked around the blanket, just looking.

No mind. Don't go there. No. Don't be under there. Illuminated only by the light from a space heater I could see something was wrapped up completely. But before the blanket was even pulled back, I knew. Deep down, I knew.

Still, I pulled it back — trying to prove otherwise, trying to break the spell.

Lying on the floor in a fetal position, his arms stretched out with his hands between his thighs — my husband. In the way he always slept. When I saw his face — still, silent, gone — something inside me shattered.

I screamed — a scream that didn't stop, a scream that tore through me, a scream that made no sound I recognized as human. I shook him. I pleaded. He didn't move. He didn't wake up. He lay there. Motionless. Lifeless.

I stumbled, shaking, blindly searching for the light switch and the door lock, but couldn't find either. In a panic, I had to crawl back out through the camper window, sobbing — no longer in control of my body. I staggered to my car, trembling violently, I lost control and urinated on myself, completely consumed by shock. This couldn't be real. It had to be a dream. It felt like an out-of-body experience — numb, hollow, incapable of comprehension.

Sitting in my car, I fumbled for the phone and called the sheriff's office. The cell service always being unreliable; I struggled to get words out through my gasping sobs. The operator struggled to understand me. Thankfully, they knew us — they pieced together my cries. Help was on its way.

I sat there, in the dark, in the cold, waiting, with a grief so big, so sharp, I thought it might swallow me whole.

Wake up Lea. Wake up.

The Calls You Never Want to Make

As I sat there, frozen in shock, trying to wrap my head around what I had just walked into, my trembling hands reached for my phone.

Tami. The first call I made was to his oldest sister in Minnesota. I don't know what I was hoping for — maybe that reaching out to her would somehow fix it, undo it, make it less real. Maybe I was reaching for a lifeline, a thread of family connection, something solid to hold onto when everything around me was shattering. Maybe she could be the one to wake him up?

When she answered, I struggled to speak. I was sobbing, choking on my own breath, forcing the words out between ragged gasps:

"Randy... dead." The only words I could get out.

There was a beat of silence on the other end — and then the sound of her screaming.

The kind of raw, guttural cry that splits the air. The sound of pure, unfiltered heartbreak crashing through a phone line. I heard her sobbing, screaming, the pain radiating across the distance between us. Then, after only a few seconds, the phone service disconnected.

I sat there staring at the phone, shaking, empty. My mind was both racing and empty all at the same time.

I tried calling my best friends, Van and Jan — the ones who had been by my side through so much, who knew our story, who knew *us*. Even though it was the middle of the night, they picked up. They didn't ask questions. They didn't press for details. All they heard was, "Randy dead." And they were on their way.

I sat there in the dark alone, waiting.

Wrapped in a silence so deep it felt crushing. No sound but the pounding of my heart, the gasping of my own breath. No comprehension, no understanding, a heavy, surreal fog of disbelief.

Then the hollering started — deep, ragged, animal sounds clawing their way out of my chest. I hit the steering wheel, over and over, the sharp crack of skin against leather filling the small space. I felt the weight of it slam into me all at once:

It was all for nothing.

All the endurance.

All the staying.

All the loving.

All the fighting.

All for nothing.

I couldn't make sense of it.

How did this happen?

How did we end up here?

How was I supposed to go on, to explain this, to live through this?

There are moments in grief that break you, that slice through everything you thought you were. This was one of them. All I could do was sit there, hollering in the dark, while the world I knew collapsed around me.

When Help Arrives, It Doesn't Heal

When the sheriff's deputies arrived, I remember watching them approach the camper cautiously, trying to open the door, trying to get a grip on the scene. Walking around. Looking in the windows. Eventually, someone broke a window and unlocked the door to get inside. Talking amongst themselves, I was comprehending their voices.

I was asked to walk over to the ambulance to be checked. I remember someone saying, "She's in shock." Hysterical, I ran from the ambulance, stumbling back to my car, desperate to call my friends again.

Why weren't they here yet? What's taking so long?

They were almost there, they'd gone to the house first, not realizing where I actually was.

When they arrived, I ran to Jan, collapsing into her, begging, *"Wake him up. Just wake him up."* I kept saying it was all for nothing.

The cold, wet ground beneath me. Her holding me trying to console me. Her trying to understand what had happened. *How did we get here?*

Everything after that is a blur.

I remember calling my sister in Texas. Begging her to wake him up. *Please wake him up.*

She tells me to call 911. I handed the phone to Jan, knowing she couldn't help. She lived too far away. My last hope to have someone wake him up. Like an act of God, make him breath again.

As Jan held the phone, someone nearby murmured, "He looks like he took a lot of drugs. A prescription overdose."

I remember the coroner arriving - backing the car up to the camper. I remember the body bag being brought out with something inside it. Thinking: *He's not in there. I didn't see them put him in the bag. He couldn't possibly be in there.*

Even today, I sometimes wonder: Was his body really in there? Is he truly gone? Or is he living another life somewhere, somehow? It's crazy, I know. But when you have no answers, your mind looks for anything to survive the weight of not knowing. The weight of being hit with a semi-truck out of nowhere.

Held Together by Shock

That night, after the chaos… after the events on the property… after the long hours of screaming and breaking — I sat on the floor of our oldest son's room, speechless.

Everything felt hollow. Not quiet — hollow. Like the air had been sucked out of the house and time itself was suspended. I opened my mouth to speak, but nothing came out. I tried again. How do you form words around the unthinkable? How do you tell your child that the world you all knew no longer exists?

I couldn't do it.

I stared at him, sobbing, my body trembling. My face must have said it all. *Help. Please help me say this. Please help me be strong enough to be the mother he needs right now.*

I look up. Van stood beside me and did what I could not. He spoke the words. I don't even remember exactly what he said — only that it shattered the stillness.

Our oldest sat frozen in disbelief. Not in dramatic outburst or denial — simply a quiet, stunned, "Okay." The kind of okay that means *I heard you, but I can't let it in yet.* The kind of okay that wraps itself around a child trying to stay upright while the earth cracks beneath him.

I dropped onto the couch, too numb to cry, too tired to think.

Not from emotion — from pure, total, cellular exhaustion. The kind of tired that doesn't live in the muscles but in the marrow. My body could no longer hold the weight of what it had just lived through.

Some strange mercy protected me that night. I hadn't been able to find the light switch in the camper, and that small delay spared me from seeing the full, bloody crime scene in vivid color. The knife, I was later told, was still lodged in his chest. Two shallow slashes across his neck. Trauma to his eye.

I didn't need to see it to carry it.

The image of him curled on the ground, motionless, his body collapsed in on itself — it was enough. It was too much.

That image alone has never left me.

It became etched in my nervous system, burned into a part of me that even time can't touch.

People think trauma is an event. However, it's also the *freeze* that follows. The mind stuck in a loop of disbelief. The body locked in survival. My soul floated above all, shattered and unable to remain inside.

I wasn't thinking in that moment — I was suspended in it. Drenched in a silence that wasn't peace. It was shock. Pure and merciless.

I didn't cry like I expected to. I didn't scream. I didn't collapse in some dramatic heap. I shut down. Because when something this devastating happens — when you're not just watching your life unravel but *living* it in real-time — your system can only take so much.

That was the beginning of *after*.

Not a chapter break. A rupture. The moment that split everything I thought I knew… into a trillion pieces.

The Mother in Me Awoke First

Van and Jan stayed with me through the night. They handled the phone calls I couldn't make. They contacted the military, notified the right people, and made sure our daughter would be sent home from the Air Force basic training. They even arranged for her husband to be flown back from Afghanistan.

They took care of it all while I slept on the couch — not peacefully, but from exhaustion so deep it felt like sinking into stone. My body had collapsed long before my mind could make sense of anything.

When I opened my eyes the next morning, I wasn't thinking about myself.

Part of me wasn't in my own body.

I was already in hers — my daughter's.

My baby girl. My husband's shadow. Daddy's girl. This would destroy her.

I didn't know how, but I felt it. Her world had just been ripped out from under her, and I couldn't stop picturing her face the moment someone told her.

I felt helpless. Panicked.

Maternal instincts collided with shock and created this strange split in me: one-part shattered wife, the other fierce, grounded mother.

Before I could even rise from the couch, Van and Jan said the words that lifted a weight I hadn't even realized I was carrying: "She's already on her way. The Red Cross is handling it. They took care of everything."

I nodded, the words floated around me, untouchable. Part of me was grateful. Part of me was frozen. Another part of me was already scanning forward — trying to anticipate what would come next. Not for her, but for everyone.

Then the next thought arrived like a jolt: *Our youngest.*

Our nine-year-old son. Still asleep upstairs. Still innocent to the reality that had torn his world in half. How do you tell a child that his father is gone? That the man who wrestled with him on the floor, who had just kissed him goodbye... would never be coming back?

I couldn't wrap my mind around it myself. How could I possibly help a child navigate what I couldn't even breathe through?

I had lost my own mother 11 years earlier, and I thought I understood what it meant to grieve a parent. This wasn't the same. That grief had a rhythm, a slow unfolding through illness and decline.

This? This was like being thrown through glass—sudden, sharp, disorienting.

There was no preparation.

No context.

No way to soften the blow.

And yet… even as my own body reeled, even as my own spirit split wide open, something ancient in me rose to the surface. The mother in me. The protector. The one who couldn't afford to fall apart yet.

Not while my children still needed me to stand. Even if that meant I had to do it with shaking hands and a fractured heart.

In the middle of all the noise and numbness, I kept thinking: *This still feels like a dream. I'm still waiting to wake up.*

Chapter Two:
The Days That Followed

"Grief is not measured in days or funerals;
it's measured in the slow, aching breaths
you take when the world expects you to keep moving."

The Days That Didn't Feel Real

To my realization, even thirteen years later, most of my memories are lost, under the protective force of my mind. Kept in value that was sealed shut as everything unfolded. Those days after his death blur together.

Not the soft, hazy kind that gently fades with time — but the kind that feels like you're living underwater, watching the world move around you while you stay suspended, breathless, and unreal.

Nothing made sense.

Time lost all shape.

The hours bled together like watercolors running down a canvas, and I couldn't tell you what happened on which day with true accuracy — or how I even moved through them.

I was functioning, though barely holding it together. I was standing. Speaking. Responding when spoken to. Inside, I was hollow. Detached. Watching life from a strange distance, as if it were happening to someone else.

I didn't cry much in those first few days. Not in the way people expect when you've just lost the love of your life. I had moments where I was completely still, even oddly calm — answering questions, signing paperwork, listening to details like it was a meeting I didn't belong in. And then, out of nowhere, I'd break.

No warning.

No slow build.

Just — cracked wide open.

The grief didn't move in waves. It moved in ambushes.

I remember thinking, *How can I feel fine and devastated at the same time? How is that even possible?*

I was walking through the motions, nodding when people spoke, letting others make decisions for me, letting them feed me, speak for me, answering the questions I didn't even understand. I couldn't guide myself, so I let others take the lead.

It wasn't surrender — it was survival.

And underneath it all was the quiet echo: *This can't be real. This can't be real. This can't be real.*

I wasn't grieving. I was displaced. Disoriented. I had no anchor, no center, no ground beneath me. Existing in a world I no longer wanted to be part of.

Everything I thought was stable had collapsed in an instant, and all that remained was the fog.

Looking back now, I see how necessary that fog was. My nervous system couldn't have survived the full weight of reality all at once. The blurriness — the unreality — it was a mercy. A cocoon. A space between collapse and confrontation.

But at the time, it didn't feel merciful.

It felt like drowning.

I couldn't even find the surface to scream.

The Interrogation

The next day, I was summoned to the sheriff's office. Not comfort. Not clarity. Not answers. Interrogation.

I remember sitting there, numb, as they asked their questions. Why this, why that, who knew what. Holding it together one minute, falling apart inconsolable the next. I remember looking at Jan as the questions kept coming, searching for answers in her face. Helpless, I thought: *Are we really here? How did we get here?*

I don't remember the conversation — only that it felt like I was no longer just the grieving wife. I was a witness. I was a suspect. An observer in the unsolved puzzle of his death. They weren't there to give me the answers I wanted, but to figure out what happened. The puzzle pieces weren't falling into place like my mind thought they should. It was like someone had mixed several puzzles together and said here, solve this.

Even though they had questions about what they observed at the scene, I was told at that time: possible suicide. *Suicide?? That can't be right.* He would never leave me and the kids this way. Through everything we went through, he wouldn't do that. To this day I still struggle wrapping my mind around that possibility. Not him. NO! He was stronger than that.

Arranging the Funeral — Arkansas

This wasn't going to be a normal funeral process. No. This was going to be a long, drawn-out process. Like our relationship, noting was ever easy. Nothing flowed like it should.

I arranged one service in Arkansas, and his family arranged another in his home state of Minnesota. Arkansas was not home for either of us. At this point, I wasn't sure if I'd stay or go back home to Texas. If I did, I couldn't leave his body all alone. I decided to send his body home to his family, where I knew loved ones would gather to pay reverence at his grave. Where a mother and father could stand at graveside and grieve losing a son so early. To have comfort knowing he was home and close.

Since losing my mother in 2002, I've come to believe the soul isn't where the physical body is. That was an empty shell of what she was. Her soul was anywhere I was.

The soul is no longer confined by the limits of the physical world. It becomes boundless — no longer tied to time and place — free to exist in all spaces, in every moment, all at once.

17

It flows through memories, lingers in places we loved, and surrounds people we cherished. In this state, the soul is not gone — it is everywhere, a quiet presence woven into the fabric of everything.

I was at peace with the decision to send his body home, and my children understood. He would always be near us no matter where we were.

His family understood and appreciated that I allowed him to go home. There was no tension, only gratitude.

A couple of years earlier, during a manic episode, he had decided to convert from lifelong Lutheran to Catholic — a decision I never fully understood. Still holding my own Catholic beliefs, I went to my church to start arrangements.

When I walked into the church to speak to the priest, I actually felt peace. I felt safe. I felt like this was going to be a place I could find some healing — a sanctuary in the middle of the chaos. Sacred. Familiar. Home. I could breathe. AHH. Something I hadn't done since I found him.

To my horror, I was told no. They wouldn't perform the service. They wouldn't allow last rites to my husband — a parishioner. Because at that point, based on what we knew, it was being called a suicide. The Catholic Church did not allow last rites for suicides.

I stood there, shocked. *What? You won't give the last rites to your own parishioner?* How does a church turn its back on you at a time like this? I was taught that even Jesus forgave the men on the cross before their death. How could the church really have this rule?

I left that meeting not with peace, but with confusion. With anger. With a deep sense of rejection that I hadn't expected. Betrayed by my own religion. The spiritual community we were part of — one that had taught love, compassion, and mercy —

had turned away. Again. And I was left holding grief, betrayal, and a thousand unanswerable questions.

Not know what to do and believing he needed his last rites, I reached out to an acquaintance, a Baptist pastor. My husband had several interactions with him over the past years when going through his panic episodes. To my relief he stepped forward and offered to perform last rites and the church ceremony my husband deserved as a Christian. Even though we weren't parishioners, he opened his arms to us. He understood. He knew this was about love and grief, not doctrine. I will forever be grateful for that act of kindness and love; I didn't care what denomination it was. My God had turned its back and slammed the door shut.

I was making calls, saying the necessary words, contacting friends — yet during it all I don't remember feeling present. It was all surreal. All a dream.

Six Days in Limbo

Because of the ongoing investigation, it took six days to get his body released from the state.

Six days.

Six days of holding space, suspended, waiting.

Six days of trying to comfort the children while trying to hold myself together on the outside.

Six days of not being able to see my husband. Not being able to confirm that this was actually happening. To confirm what my mind and heart were screaming was merely a dream — an alternate reality I wasn't living, stuck in limbo.

A couple of days after his passing, I met with our friend Mark. He was not only our dear friend, he was also the funeral home owner and the county coroner. I remember him saying this had been one of the hardest autopsies and body preparations he had ever had to do. For whatever act of mercy, Mark was not on call the night I found my husband. He wasn't the one to remove his body from the camper. To see the scene. To carry those memories. I couldn't fathom preparing a body for someone you called a friend, whose daughters played ball together. The agony of telling me everything he found and suspected. That is where my heart breaks for his part of our story.

We sat and started organizing. I was fortunate — Mark on one side, Jan on the other. My daughter in the corner and his sister nearby. Jan never left my side. Walking with me step by step. Leaving work when I needed the extra support. Making the decisions I couldn't, while I numbly agreed. I heard the words although I couldn't comprehend what they were saying. Like a foreign language I hadn't learned yet was supposed to know. I knew I was in good hands — people who loved us deeply and only wanted the best. They wouldn't guide me wrong. We were family. Not by blood — by spirit.

It was at this point I realized:

I can't do this.

My nervous system was overloaded. I didn't have the strength or mental capacity to do this. I had to call my doctor for a prescription — something to help me survive this, to help me get through the decisions, the grief, the loss. Something to help numb the emptiness I felt. If that was even possible. To hold back the anguish that was closing in on me.

The Casket

We went back to the funeral home to choose the casket. I'm not sure which day, yet I recollect I couldn't even walk through the door on this day.

I drove up to the front of the building. I exited my car and walked to the door. I reached for the handle and something inside me shattered. I broke down — earth shattering sobbing right there on the steps. My body shacking. The sound tore out of me without permission, raw and guttural, like my body was trying to expel a grief too big to hold inside.

It was time to pick the casket.

Time to pick the container, the vessel, the box that would hold the body of the man I had loved.

My best friend and companion of twenty-five years.

Time to make decisions I never wanted to face. And I didn't have the strength. We had our whole future ahead of us still.

My mind spiraled: *No. No. If I don't do this, it's not happening. If I just stand here, if I freeze here, if I refuse to cross the threshold — maybe it all stops. Maybe none of this becomes real.*

Finally, with trembling hands, I forced myself inside. I sat down heavily, shaking, barely able to breathe. Someone handed me a pill and a glass of water — the only thing that would quiet the hurricane of panic inside me long enough to let me function, to let me survive these next unbearable steps.

Everything felt foggy, surreal, like moving through a dream I desperately wanted to wake up from.

When I stood up, I could feel my legs resisting — stiff, unsteady, like they were trying to root me to the floor, to keep me from walking into the next layer of pain.

I took one step. Then another. Then another.

I walked slowly, deliberately, down the hall to the room that housed the caskets. The final resting bed for so many to follow.

Hyperventilating.

Whispering to myself between gasps, *Calm. Breathe. Calm. Breathe.* Telling myself, *It's okay. You can do this. You have to do this.*

2̇

Jan was right there, one hand on my back, the other holding my arm, anchoring me with her presence. Without her, I don't know if I could have kept moving.

We reached the door of the casket room. I placed my hand on the doorframe as if bracing for the train to hit. Glancing inside and seeing all the caskets lined up against the walls.

I stopped.

Body shaking. Heart racing. Breath catching in my throat.

It's okay. It's okay. You're strong.

And then — somehow — I stepped inside. The overwhelm hit me like a tidal wave. The reality of it. The unbearable *realness* of standing in a room full of caskets, knowing that one of them was for *him*. For the man I had built a life with, dreamed a future with, fought through storms with. For the man whose laugh I could still hear in the back of my mind, whose scent still clung to the clothes at home.

I wish I could remember more details, but I can't. I can't remember actually seeing the caskets outside the glace at the door. I can't remember hearing the differences between them or why I chose the one I did. I can't even picture in my head what the one I chose looked like unless I see a picture. It's all a blur, a haze of survival and numbness. I only know that, somehow, I made the decisions that had to be made.

I chose the casket. The final place his body would rest for eternity. The vessel that would hold what was left of the life we shared, the dreams we had, the man I loved.

I did it. Step by step. Breath by breath. With a heart breaking but still beating, barley.

The First Sight

I don't know what was harder — actually finding his body that night or seeing him lying in his casket, lifeless, for the first time. Coming to grips with the reality of what was actually happening. A life with him no longer in it.

Walking up to the funeral home door again, dreading this next phase. Still disbelieving. Still walking through the steps without comprehending. *Don't open that door. Turn around now and go home. He's home, waiting for me.* The panic setting in. The struggle to breathe. Saying aloud: *I can't do this. I can't do this. No, no, I can't.*

Finally, sitting in the lobby.

Trying to calm down.

Trying to breathe. Struggling to suppress the rising panic, but it overwhelms me — a tidal wave too immense to hold back. Jan at my side, allowing me time, letting me know it was okay.

Eventually, I was guided into the viewing room, slowly, cautiously. Looking down at the ground as I stepped two feet in, then looking up. Squeezing my eyes closed.

No!

Everything in me broke, and I crumbled.

My legs gave out.

My body went limp.

I hit the floor.

Crying uncontrollably. Inconsolable. Cries you can't understand unless you've felt them yourself. Unless you've been witness to such a deep level of grief and disbelief.

Disbelief.

Denial.

My mind trying to protect me from the unimaginable. *This isn't happening. That's not him. This is a lie.*

It took several minutes to gain control enough to stand.

Looking to the ground again, I was guided to the side of his casket. As I timidly looked up to gaze upon his body, again I collapsed — nearly pulling over the casket as I hit the floor. It was too overwhelming. Too much to handle.

My mind wanted to go into utter denial: *No. I didn't see them take the body out of the camper. I didn't see them put his body in the body bag. This isn't him. His face is too narrow. His strong features are gone. That's not my husband.*

What else is the mind to do when you don't want to accept what is right in front of you? You deny with every part of your essence. Deep to your inner core.

And it's all hazy once more. Pain-clouded recollections, sealed away by a mind trying to protect itself. A love and grief so deep it still protects me now.

The Arkansas Funeral

The day of the Arkansas funeral came. A quiet, eerie feel settled over the house as we dressed, preparing for the first service.

I'm going to be strong. I'm going to be strong, I kept repeating, moving almost in a daze. Walking inside a living dream I couldn't wake up from.

Me. Our three children. My dad. His oldest sister. My son-in-law.

The only family present in our time of need.

Three of my four siblings chose not to attend. I was never given a reason. They just didn't come. I guess they felt it wasn't worth their time to support their baby sister in her time of need.

I felt abandoned by my own family — and his. I felt sorry for my children, that they didn't have anyone else there to love them like I did. Alone. *How does family turn their back?* I still don't understand.

Arriving at the church, Van and Jan were waiting for us. As I walked through the entrance reality finally hit. I was instantly thrown back to truth a still wanted to deny. My husband was dead.

Panic attack.

I couldn't breathe.

Hyperventilating.

Sobbing.

Nearly buckling to the ground.

Saying *No. No. I can't do this.*

The heartache. The future. The dreams. All gone.

I was alone. He had left me.

They walked me to a chair on the side. I took a pill to calm me, to numb me from reality. After a few minutes, it was time to start. Surrounded and being guided, I was led to the front.

All I wanted to do was stream to the heavens, "God, why?" Instead, I clenched my fist, raised them in the air, and let out a silent scream through tightly shut lips. *I want it all to stop. Just stop. Roll back time. Let me stop this nightmare.* My daughter is next to me, trying to correct my unacceptable behavior. I didn't care how I was acting. My sorrow overrode any socially unacceptable behavior being observed.

As the medication took hold I calmed. Able to finally feel a breath. My heart returning to my chest. Panic subsiding.

It was a heartfelt service. Wonderful stories of memories. Words of love and laughter. Tears of sorrow.

With measured grace, the Military Honor Guard carried his casket, the weight of silence heavier than the flag it bore. The ceremonial folding of the flag draping his casket. I was going through the motions, playing my part in my own shattered reality.

Then — it was time to go outside.

The gun salute.

The presentation of his flag.

A surreal moment.

As we gathered outside, the gunshots erupted, and my body convulsed with a cry I couldn't contain. Another shot — and I was shaking, weeping from a place beyond words. Crying from the depths of my heart. Agony to my core. This was beyond difficult. The depth of pain.

The realization. The anger. The love. All wound up together, released in each scream.

Finally silence.

Then I heard it — that unmistakable tap of military shoes, each step drawing nearer. I knew that sound. My husband had those shoes that made that distinct sound.

Click.

Click.

Click.

I know why they are getting closer. My husband had performed this same honor at other military funerals. And now, it's being done for him.

Standing before me was one of the Honor Guard guardsmen, holding his pristinely folded flag and reciting the presentation speech. He handed me the flag, and I couldn't bring myself to take it. I reached halfway out and pulled my arms back — once, twice, three times.

I can't do it. No, I don't want it. It's too final.

At my side, I hear my sweet friend from work whisper, *Lea, you have to take it.*

I finally reached out as the flag was slowly and reverently placed in my arms followed by a salute. I embraced it. Holding it to my chest. Tears flowing down my cheeks.

It was followed by three rifle shells that had been shot in his memory. Shots that will never leave my ears. Shots that end up pulling me back to this exact moment during my fathers military salute years later.

Back in the church, I remember sitting there as everyone filed through the front of the church to say their final goodbyes and offer their condolences. I remember speaking to a few friends. Saying the right words, smiling, and trying to hold it together.

Before leaving, I spoke to Mark to ensure his body was getting to the airport to transport to Minnesota next. The next leg of his journey.

Once again, the rest fades — a fog, a closing curtain, the mind sealing itself to protect what the heart can no longer bear.

Chapter Three:
Minnesota — The Second Burial

"They lowered his body into the ground —
but it was my soul that got buried alive."

Final Goodbyes

After the Arkansas funeral, there was no rest. No pause. No breath. No time to grieve properly.

There was still another service waiting for us — another goodbye, another weight to carry, another layer of sorrow to shoulder when we were already drained. We rented a van so we could all ride together — me, my three children, my daughter's husband, and my dad. My dad, the father with whom I hadn't shared a close or easy relationship growing up, now stood by my side through it all, refusing to let me face this alone. His presence was steady, surprising, and deeply needed.

We headed north, mile after mile, through the winter-gray landscape, the van filled with quiet, exhaustion, and the heaviness of what we were traveling toward. We were on our way to another viewing, another service, another round of people gathering to mourn, to remember, to say the words we were all running out of: I'm so sorry. I'm so sorry. I'm so sorry.

Our final goodbyes.

There were moments when I felt like I was moving through it all in a haze, placing one foot in front of the other because that's what was required. Under that numbness was a raw, unrelenting ache — the ache of knowing that no matter how many ceremonies, no matter how many graveside prayers, there would never be a closure big enough to hold all the loss we were carrying Especially when you don't know why.

This was more than a goodbye. It was the start of a long, challenging journey I never wanted to take—at least not at age 43. There were still years of a future ahead of us, and yet somehow, I knew I'd have to find a way to keep moving forward regardless.

Sending Him Home

Arranging his transport is one of those things I only vaguely remember — like walking through a mist, every moment clouded by shock and exhaustion. I know I signed forms, nodded at decisions, gave permission — but the details live behind a mist I can barely access.

Thanks to Mark, our funeral director, everything was handled with a grace I couldn't have summoned myself. Mark made the calls. He filed the paperwork. He coordinated with the receiving funeral home up north. I didn't have to navigate the bureaucracy of death; I only had to survive it.

He had prepared his body, sending instructions to the other funeral home not to attempt any touch-ups. He ensured the clothing around the neck was arranged to conceal the scars. Ensured the necessary documentation was transferred for a smooth transition.

I only know it all got done because, somehow, when we arrived in Minnesota, he was there. His family was waiting on their end — waiting for their son, their brother, their uncle to come home one last time. They understood why I wanted him buried there. They appreciated it. There was no conflict, only a collective grief that outweighed any differences among us.

There's something sobering about realizing that, in death, the arguments, the distances, the differences fall away. What's left is only the ache, only the finality, only the deep human need to make sure the person you loved — no matter how complicated that love was — is laid to rest with dignity, with care, with belonging.

So, we sent him home. We carried the memory of him across the miles, across the weight of all the unfinished conversations, the unresolved tensions, the dreams that would never come to pass. We sent him home to the place his family still held open for him — a place that would now carry his name, his memory, his resting presence.

Arriving in Minnesota

Arriving in Minnesota was a strange, almost surreal mix of numbness and sharp, piercing pain. The biting cold hung heavy in the air, while dirty snow piled up along the edges of the street — gray and slushy from days of neglect. The faint crunch underfoot echoed in the quiet, a harsh reminder of winter's stubborn grip.

The cold was deep, bone-aching — wrapping around me like a heavy, unwelcome cloak. Snow lay thick on the ground, soft in some places, hardened and gray in others where plows had piled it high. Snowbanks lined the old streets like silent walls, stark evidence of Minnesota's long, unrelenting winter.

Above, the sky hung low and overcast, pressing down on the landscape — and on my chest. The air was still, not peaceful. It was weighted, somber — the kind of stillness that makes you painfully aware of every breath, every footstep, every memory crowding in around you.

On the one hand, I was drained. I was physically, emotionally, spiritually, down to the marrow of my bones. I had already been through so much: finding him, the funeral in Arkansas, the military salute, the endless faces in the church, the sympathetic words, the heavy burden of managing two funeral expenses, two sets of logistics, two places where he belonged. I was running on fumes, barely holding myself upright much less present.

On the other hand, the moment I stepped into his parents' home, the moment I saw his family's faces, heard their voices, smelled the familiar air of a house we had visited so many times

— it was like a blade sliding under my skin, reopening wounds I didn't even know were still bleeding. It wasn't the peace I had hoped for in being there. Instead, the harsh reality of shared memories crashed over me like a wave.

This wasn't my home, but it was his.

The rooms we had shared when we visited, the bed where we stayed, the little everyday corners filled with his echoes — they were waiting there, untouched, as if he might walk back in at any moment.

I saw the backyard where we had once sat around a campfire, laughing with his family, where he had stood tall and sure in the flickering light. I saw the kitchen where his mother had cooked us meals, where his father had poured coffee, where voices had once mixed in conversation.

And standing there, I felt like I was carrying two separate lives inside me. The one we had built together — the home, the family, the plans, the future we fought so hard to shape in Arkansas — and the one he had come from, the history that had shaped him long before I entered his world.

This Minnesota life had been waiting quietly in the background. Not always spoken, not always front and center, nevertheless always there — woven into him, inseparable from who he was.

I remember feeling both surrounded and isolated. Part of the family but somehow hovering outside. Grieving not only the man I had lost, the intertwining of all his worlds — the parts of him that belonged here, to this land, this family, these people. And realizing, with a hollow ache, that I was now a thread stretched between two places, two versions of him, two layers of goodbye. I belonged by name, not by blood.

Family Dynamics

Being there, surrounded by his family, was complicated. They were kind, they were loving — however they were grieving in their own way. Their loss was not the same as mine. They had lost a son, a brother, a childhood friend. I had lost a partner, a co-parent, a future.

We were all mourning the same man, but we were standing in different worlds. I felt like an outsider. I didn't belong without him standing beside me. He was my validation to the family. He is what connected us.

I remember his parents wanting him buried in the family plot — again, we ran into the same religious roadblocks we had faced in Arkansas. Religious rules that made no sense.

Because of his conversion to Catholicism, the Lutheran church refused to allow him to be buried on their side of the cemetery—no exceptions. They would oversee the mass, but that was the extent of their involvement.

By that point, I'd had enough of the religious bureaucracy. I didn't care anymore. I told the family he hadn't completed his final Catholic teachings—he was still Lutheran.

I straight up lied.

I lied for him.

I lied for his parents.

The Catholic Church had turned its back on me — and I now turned my back on it.

I don't feel guilty.

I won't apologize.

I won't ask for penance.

A quiet deception — but it let him rest where he belonged, with his family. Only his oldest sister knew the truth — until now.

As we sat in the kitchen, reviewing the service and sorting out the details, I was blindsided out of nowhere. I was told, most emphatically, that I would not be allowed to place a rosary in his hands.

Wait... what? I wasn't allowed to place a rosary in his hands? The words hit me like a punch to the gut. The church wouldn't allow it — nothing was permitted in the casket except the flag. It felt like a final, cruel barrier, stripping away even the smallest comfort or gesture of faith.

I was fuming—boiling over with rage. Screaming and hollering at the family, my voice cracking under the weight of it all. Beyond angry. Exhausted to my core. Tired of people laying down stupid rules like chains, telling me what couldn't be done, like we had no say, no room for grace or compassion. Every word felt like another blow, draining the last bit of strength I had left.

I was done. It was the last blow I could take.

We packed our things and found a hotel for the remainder of our time there. I needed space. I needed to breathe. I needed... him back. I needed my husband more than anything else at that point.

The Minnesota Services

The Minnesota services unfolded in their own way—each moment carrying a rhythm unfamiliar yet heavy with meaning. Visitation. Funeral service. Graveside. Each step felt like moving through a carefully choreographed ritual, one shaped by traditions that weren't mine.

A different church.

A different pastor.

A different circle of mourners.

It was like watching someone else's story unfold, a story filled with grief yet distant from my own. I stood there, an outsider caught between memories and strangers, feeling the weight of loss in a place that didn't quite feel like home.

I remember arriving at the funeral home for the visitation, stepping into a sea of people. We pushed our way through the crowd, each step heavier than the last. I hadn't spoken or seen the family since I left the house.

I found myself standing at the casket — frozen in place, a surge of betrayal crashing over me.

Pinned to the cloth inside the casket were random items — tokens, keepsakes placed by the very people who had told me I couldn't lay a rosary in his hands. The hypocrisy stung sharply, fueling a fire of anger that churned deep inside. How could they decide what was allowed, what wasn't? It wasn't the church's decision; it was the families. My frustration and grief tangled together, a bitter knot tightening with every breath.

Betrayed. Lied to, after all I had done to ensure he was home and buried in the family plot. I stayed quiet. Until this moment, I stayed quiet. Never mentioning a word. That betrayal runs deep.

It wasn't only about a rosary or what was pinned to the lining of the casket. It was about control — about being silenced in a moment that should have belonged to all of us. It was about grief being filtered through rules and gatekeeping, while I stood there feeling shut out of my own goodbye. That moment carved something sharp into me, something that still aches when I think about it.

I recall standing in the receiving line next to his dad, listening, half inside my body and half hovering somewhere above it. I remember looking at my children, watching them grieve quietly, their faces tight and pale. I remember shaking hands with people whose names I instantly forgot.

The words echoed in my mind, hollow and desperate. I felt disconnected, like my body was present but my mind had slipped somewhere far away. The hum of voices around me faded into the background, replaced by the thudding silence of disbelief. I wanted to reach for him, to wake him up, to rewind time. All I could do was stand there — still, numb, and quietly breaking.

I held his hand.

It surprised me — how warm it still was, as if he were sleeping, still with me somehow. For a moment, I let myself believe it.

I embraced that warmth, holding onto it like it could keep him here a little longer.

Just one more moment.

One more breath.

I asked someone to find me a lint brush so I could clean the dirt off his blue military uniform.

He was military. It had to be perfect. He would've accepted anything less.

I straightened his name tag—carefully, precisely. Then I smoothed his hair, making sure every detail was right.

It was the last act of service I could offer him; the only thing left within my control.

I sat next to my dad, holding his hand, staring towards the casket for what felt like eternity.

Watching my father cry, hearing him whisper that my husband was like a son to him. It was difficult to witness the anguish on his face and in his voice — but it was healing, too. Support between us, when I had least expected it.

The next day was the final mass. The last goodbyes. The last time I would see his physical body.

I don't remember getting ready that morning. I don't remember arriving at the church or even sitting through the service. It's all a blur now, tucked away in the shadowed caverns of my mind, obscured by the heavy fog of shock and bone-deep exhaustion. The only thing I remember is the closing of the casket.

When it was time to close the casket, people passed by one by one, offering their final goodbyes.

There were tears — quiet, shaking, uncontrollable. Some whispered parting words. Others placed a hand on the casket and walked away, too broken to speak. Like me, they were struggling—each of us lost in our own silence, trying to make sense of something that never would.

I was the last one to say goodbye.

The room had quieted, the crowd had thinned, but I stayed — my hand resting on the edge of the casket, unwilling to let go.

This was it. The final moment. Somehow, no matter how long I stood there, it still wasn't long enough.

With my dad's personal rosary in hand, and him by my side, we placed it gently into my husband's hands.

I'll be damned if he goes without one. I didn't care what the rules were. He was Catholic by choice — and I would honor that decision.

Placing the rosary in his hands wasn't tradition; it was sacred. A final ritual that mattered. A quiet symbol of the faith he had chosen, the peace he had sought.

To deny him that would have been a betrayal.

So ,I did what I knew was right. I gracefully bestowed the rosary into his hands — because it belonged there, because he would have wanted it there.

It was more than a simple gesture. It was an act of defiance. Defiance against the rigidity of organized religion, against the silence that tried to dictate what grief should look like, against the family that said I couldn't.

But above all, it was an act of loyalty — fierce, unapologetic love. The quiet defiance of two people refusing to let him go without the dignity he deserved and the religion he willingly chose.

The Burial

At the graveside, something inside me cracked again. Reality. There is no dream. Time isn't going back. There is no magical wand. We are here. Now. Actually doing the unimaginable: laying my husband to rest far too soon.

I remember hearing *Taps* play softly from a distant speaker — each note hanging in the cold air, heavy with sorrow and finality. Then came another gun salute — sharp, solemn cracks echoing through the stillness, each shot marking a final farewell.

I recall watching his parents, seated next to each other, being presented yet another flag that had been draped over his casket — an honor wrapped in folds of grief and pride, a silent testament to a life and sacrifice that words couldn't fully capture. Knowing the agony and emptiness of acceptance. Knowing he would never walk through the door again. No more smiles. No more kisses. Just gone.

Once the graveside service was over, I lingered. Friends and family all returning to their cars, ready to leave, watching me.

Waiting in their warm vehicles — *What is she going to do next?* In quiet observation.

I couldn't bring myself to walk away just yet. The chapter wasn't quite complete. There is something so brutally final about watching a casket lowered into the ground. It's not the service, not the prayers, not the eulogies — it's that moment when you realize: *I can't touch him anymore. I can't go back. He's not waking up ever again.*

Emptiness.

Pure soul level emptiness.

I remember standing there, feeling the cold bite of the wind, watching the casket go down. I remember my hands clenching, my body shaking — not from the cold and snow, but from a place I never want touched again. The deepest core of my existence.

I watched as they lowered the casket — each inch it sank felt like a piece of my own soul being buried alongside it. The weight of loss pressed down on me, hollowing out the space where hope once lived.

In that moment, I was shattered and utterly alone, stripped of the part of myself that had walked beside him. It was more than grief — it was the loss of who I was, a quiet devastation that echoed in the silence left behind.

It was at that moment I knew — I was no longer that person who had wrapped the last 25 years of her life around him.

He had been the center, my anchor through every storm, every joy, every battle we fought side by side. No matter what we endured, in the end, it always came back to us — together, unbreakable. Nothing could ever severe the bond we shared.

Until now. Until death.

Now, that *us* was gone.

And with it, the person I thought I was — complete, connected, whole — shattered into something new and unrecognizable. A shell of my former self. Never to be the same again.

I sat on the frozen ground, not even phased. Numbness had set in. I took a handful of frozen earth. Threw it into the hole on top of the burial vault that housed his casket. Ashes to ashes. Dust to dust.

Sitting by the graveside as the last handful of earth hit the burial vault, hearing the dull thud, graveyard workers waiting for me to leave, feeling the chill in the air press into my skin — that was when it landed even harder: this is final. This is real. There is no one coming to fix this.

Crying alone.

Saying my final goodbye.

I brought him home. I kept my promise. Why do I feel emptier, not less?

I struggled to get up to leave.

I wanted to stay forever.

I wanted him back.

I wanted time to rewind.

More than anything, I wanted my children to have their father back.

When I walk away from here, I'm not only leaving the cemetery. I'm leaving a chapter of my life that will never return. I'm stepping into a world I don't recognize. A world I never asked for.

Yet, somehow, with trembling steps, I stood up and turned. I walked to the car. I buckled my seatbelt. We drove away, carrying every last goodbye inside me, knowing that some parts of me — the parts that were only his — would always, always stay there.

After the Cemetery

After the cemetery, there was no great moment of relief. There was no cinematic closure. There were quiet cars pulling away from the cemetery, small clusters of family heading back to the church, sandwiches waiting on kitchen counters, awkward conversations murmured over coffee.

I remember standing at the church hall, watching everyone peels away, each step they took feeling like another layer of my world falling away. I remember sitting in a chair later, eating, staring out the window, thinking I have no idea what comes next. I physically survived the funerals. But I hadn't survived the grief. That was beginning.

The leaving — that was when it hit the hardest. Driving back to Arkansas, without him for the first time ever.

He wasn't by my side. He wasn't at home waiting for me.

His body was in his casket in an eternal sleep.

I didn't want to leave.

Leaving felt like betrayal.

Leaving felt like abandoning him.

Leaving felt like crossing over a line I couldn't uncross — from being a wife who was grieving, to being a widow who had to figure out what life meant without him. To figure out who I was now.

What Stayed with Me

Even now, when I look back on Minnesota, it's like flipping through a photo album where numerous pages are missing. Certain moments are crystal clear — the sound of the wind at the graveside, the feel of the cold on my body, the moment his parents received the flag. The rest is hazy, wrapped in the protective fog my mind put up to shield me.

It was supposed to be closure. But it didn't feel like closure.

It felt like one more door closing behind me — and an empty, lonely road ahead.

Even now, years later, the echoes of that burial live inside me. Not as sharp pain, not as raw grief, but as a quiet weight, a permanent imprint on the shape of my soul.

It taught me that closure is not a single event. It's not a funeral or a folded flag or a graveside prayer. Closure is a long, winding road, one you walk slowly, one you stumble down and rise again from, one you carry with you, even as life begins — somehow, some way — to move forward.

Sometimes, closure isn't really closure at all.

It's not a neat ending or a clean break. It doesn't magically heal the wounds or erase the ache. Instead, it's more like the slow, often painful internalization of a new reality — where you don't accept what's happened, but absorb it, letting it reshape the very core of who you are.

Closure can be messy, incomplete, and slow to come— sometimes it comes in moments, brief flickers of peace that are quickly overshadowed by fresh waves of grief.

It's less about "moving on" and more about learning to carry the loss, to live alongside it, even when the emptiness feels like it might swallow you whole.

Because in truth, some parts of us never fully close — they stay open, raw, and alive, a testament to what was lost and what will never be forgotten.

Chapter Four:
Coming Home to an Empty Life

*"When the house falls silent, grief finds its loudest voice —
echoing through every room you thought you knew."*

The house was quiet when we returned. Too quiet. Hollow

After the funerals, after the flights, after the cars were unpacked, after the last goodbyes, the only thing left was silence. It's the kind of silence that makes it uncomfortable to sit alone in a room — because it's *too* quiet, filled not with peace, but with the weight of everything left unsaid and undone.

I remember walking through the front door and realizing: *There's no one waiting for me here*. Not him. Not his laugh, his arms, his smell, his voice. Not even the awful cigarette smoke I detested yet wish I could smell again. Now, it was nothing more than a house. A shell.

The Layered Emptiness

It wasn't simply his absence. It was everything else that was happening as well — like a series of aftershocks following the earthquake of his death.

In November 2012, four months before he died, our daughter got married. I watched her step into her own adult life, happy and bittersweet all at once. She left for Air Force basic training, carving out her own path, her own future. I was happy for her, truly — but her absence left a space, a quietness in the house where her laughter and presence had always been.

Then, in August 2013, five months after his death, our oldest son graduated from college and moved away to attend school. Another chapter closing, another piece of our family stretching out into the world. So very proud he was chasing his own dreams, as he should, however I felt the sting of his departure like a second loss layered on top of the first. I struggled with him leaving yet supported him every bit on the outside. He was stepping into himself.

Suddenly, it wasn't just that my husband was gone. It was that the family I had poured myself into for so many years — the people I had centered my days, my time, my love around — were scattering.

Room by room, person by person, the house emptied. Her bedroom left with only soft outlines where her things had been. His room, once lively and full of plans, now silent. The living room, once full of the hustle and noise of comings and goings, no longer filled by conversation and movement. The echoes in the house grew louder with each goodbye.

There I stood, in the middle of it all. Holding the weight. Holding the bills. Holding the silence. Holding the grief. Just me and our youngest child.

It was a layered emptiness — not the absence of one person, but the unraveling of a whole life. I had been the center, the glue, the one who kept everything humming in the background. Now, I was the one left to face the quiet, to carry the sorrow, to wonder what came next when every familiar role had been stripped away.

It wasn't simply the loss of my husband — it was the loss of the family rhythm, the loss of the daily noise and motion, the loss of the life I had known. I wasn't grieving him. I was grieving the life we had all shared — and the woman I had been within it.

Financial Collapse

As if losing him wasn't enough, the financial blow came crashing in quickly. The loss of his income sent everything tumbling, turning the situation into an avalanche I wasn't prepared for.

There were the funeral expenses — two services, two funerals, two states.

There were the lingering bills.

The house.

The boat.

The property.

The truck.

The dreams we had built together, all tied up in payments and paperwork.

My husband had been the primary earner. We needed two sources of income to support our home and family. I knew without his income it would be impossible for us to stay in the house. But knowing it didn't make it easier to accept.

Many sleepless nights were had wondering what I was supposed to do. Where do we go? How do you adjust from 1.5 acres to an apartment? How will my son manage. He's lost so much already.

When he was alive, even when things were hard, we had each other. No matter what, we always knew we'd have each other. We made plans together. We dreamed together. We fought for the future together.

After he was gone, everything began to collapse.

There were no more *we* decisions—only *me*, staring down bills, choices, responsibilities we were supposed to face together.

I couldn't hold it all. I tried. But the weight was relentless.

The money wasn't there. What had once been manageable with two incomes, two people, two hearts carrying the load — now felt impossible.

Every envelope that arrived in the mail felt like a threat. Every decision became a triage of what could wait, what might break, what would slip through the cracks, what I was willing to lose next.

Underneath it all was the deeper truth: I wasn't just grieving him — I was grieving the life we built, the security we had, the future we planned for.

It all unraveled. Quietly. Brutally.

Eventually, I reached a breaking point. My body was drained. My heart emptied. My spirit broken. The stress and pressure of trying to keep it all together crushed me. I was done.

Just six months after his death, I caved and filed for Chapter 13 bankruptcy.

It nearly destroyed what was left of me.

I felt like a failure. Like I had let everyone down. That somehow, this meant I had mismanaged our life, squandered our finances, and made irresponsible choices. I imagined what people would think — that I had been reckless or frivolous. That I should have known better. That I should have been stronger.

The truth was, I wasn't careless. I wasn't extravagant. I was a grieving widow trying to keep my son's world from falling apart while mine already had.

I filed because I was desperate. Because I wanted stability for my son. Because I wanted to protect the home we built, the memories we made, the future we had once imagined — sitting on the back porch, watching our grandchildren play.

It was a dream I had prayed for, for years. A place where my two older children had finally found roots — no longer fearing the upheaval of another military move.

However, in the end, not even love or memory was enough to keep the walls standing.

For the next five long months, I scraped and stretched— counting coins, watching every dollar, holding my breath every time a bill arrived in the mail. I did everything I could to make it work, to keep us afloat, to hold on just a little longer.

But even Chapter 13 couldn't lift the weight. The house payment alone was crushing on a single income.

In the end, I surrendered — not out of weakness, but because I had nothing left to give. I was wrung dry.

Letting go wasn't a choice. It was survival.

I filed Chapter 7.

I gave up.

I walked away from the house, the boat, the property, his truck — from the life we had built, from the memories, from the future plans.

I left with the contents of our home, my car, and the memories sealed inside me.

How do you go from a family of five, a beautiful home, plans, a future — to standing at your car, everything you have left packed, the home empty, your youngest child beside you?

How did this happen?

How did I get here?

The Emotional Unraveling

People talk about grief like it's a single thing. A singular event. A death, a funeral, a mourning period — and then, somehow, you move forward. You go back to work. You go back to errands. You go back to the business of living, as if grief is a chapter you close.

That's not how it was for me.

Grief wasn't a wave; it was a flood. And the flood didn't just hit once, sweeping through and then receding. It came in relentless surges, again and again, crashing over every corner of my life, soaking into every crack I tried to seal up.

Grief was not gentle. It didn't whisper. It stormed in. It gave me no room to breathe, no chance to come up for air.

It would hit me like a freight train—sudden, violent, and without warning. Over and over again.

When I thought I could catch my breath, when I finally saw the faintest glimmer of light, it would come barreling back out of nowhere — flattening me all over again.

It hit in the mornings, when the house was too quiet. When the air felt thick with absence, when even the sunlight seemed to fall differently across the kitchen floor.

It hit hardest at night — when the bed felt too heavy without his weight beside me, when I reached out instinctively in the dark only to touch emptiness, when the silence was deafening without the snores that used to irritate me and keep me up all night.

Grief lived in those quiet hours, where memory and absence tangled together in the dark.

It hit when I walked into the sheriff's office or sat across from the lawyer going over details I could barely absorb.

It hit when I packed boxes I never wanted to pack, when I signed over deeds to places that held our laughter, our arguments, our memories.

It hit when I watched my daughter board a plane, stepping into her military life, her dreams, her distance.

It hit when I helped my son load his things into a car, his future packed into boxes, waving bye as he pulled away.

Every goodbye — every single one — was layered on top of the goodbye that mattered most. Every departure, every loss, every shift felt like another thread tugged loose, unraveling the life I had spent years sewing together with love, with sacrifice, with belief.

The nights were the worst. That's when the questions circled like vultures — why, how, what if? My brain replayed every conversation, every moment, desperate for a clue. I was haunted by grief. I was haunted by his image on the floor that wouldn't leave my head. I was haunted by the gaping silence of an unfinished investigation.

This wasn't grief as a chapter. This was grief as a storm system, circling and circling, reshaping everything in its path.

Today the weight of an unsolved case carries a different level of grief. The grief of not knowing why and who. To never know the reason his life was extinguished. A chapter that will never be closed for me or my children. Like the author decided to stop writing.

I went through the stages of grief — but not neatly, not one step at a time like the books or therapists say. I titrated through all of them like droplets of water hitting a hot skillet. No rhyme. No reason.

Denial, anger, bargaining, depression, acceptance — sometimes all within the same hour. Acceptance for a moment, then red-hot anger the next.

Thinking: The body in the casket wasn't him. There were resemblances, but it didn't fully look like him. Maybe he's not truly dead. Maybe this is all a mistake.

Walking in a daze, moving through the motions, disengaged, barely tethered to the ground beneath my feet.

And no one tells you that when the storm moves in, you don't walk away untouched — you come out on the other side a different person, fractured by held together by survival, by sorrow, by a strength you never wanted to need.

A strength I never knew I possessed.

This is the emotional unraveling I carry with me — not as a wound that defines me, but as a truth I honor. A truth that says: I have been torn open. And somehow, I am still here.

Tough Love, and the Question I Still Carry

There's a truth I have rarely spoken aloud — not because I wanted to hide it, but because I didn't know where it fit inside the story. It is a detail so sharp, so tangled in guilt and grief, that even now, years later, I sometimes hold it like a boulder in my pocket, too heavy to fully put down.

In Arkansas, once a divorce is filed, you have 18 months to finalize it before it expires. We were almost at the end of that window. On February 13, 2013 — one day before the deadline — we signed the final paperwork. Not because I wanted to walk away. Not because I had stopped loving him. Because I was desperate.

It was my last desperate act — tough love.

I wanted him to understand how serious this was — how much his untreated bipolar disorder and alcohol addiction were ripping through our family, through our marriage, through the man I knew he was beneath the illness.

Filing for divorce wasn't a rejection; it was a final plea.

It was the strongest push I had left to make him face the help he needed. I thought, maybe, just maybe, this would wake him up.

I remember sitting in the car after signing the papers and him saying, "I know you can't give me anymore chances".

I sat there, looking at him through tears, and said, "I'd do Mom's funeral a thousand times over, all by myself, before ever wanting to do *this*."

He understood. He didn't say a word — he didn't have to. The weight of it was already known between us.

I was his rock. His safety net. The one who was always there — no matter how unpredictable things got between us, no matter how messy life became.

We were connected in a way no one else could fully understand. It was deeper than love, deeper than struggle. It was something unspoken, something rooted in years of surviving together, of choosing each other again and again — even when it wasn't easy.

The finalized papers were sitting in the mailbox the day he died. Signed. Sealed. Done. As if life had drawn a line in ink just hours before it ended in blood.

I remember holding them in my hands, numb, wondering — *Did he see them?*

Did he open the mailbox that morning?

Did he hold them?

Read them?

The thought has gutted me since. Was that the last thing he touched from me — cold, final paperwork instead of warmth, instead of grace?

The timing felt too cruel to be coincidence. Like some twisted irony the universe had delivered with a smirk.

That detail haunts me. It's always there, unyielding.

Was it my fault?

Did I push too hard?

Did I pull away when I should have drawn closer?

Did my last-ditch attempt to save us become the final fracture?

The hardest question — the one that still won't let me go: *Was I the reason my children no longer have a father?*

Am I to blame?

These are the questions no one can answer — not the sheriff, not the coroner, not the counselors, not the clergy, not even myself. These are the questions I have had to carry inside my own heart, in the rawest corners of my grief.

I know, on some rational level, that I am not responsible for his death. That his pain, his struggles, his choices were his own. That the illness he battled may have been bigger than either of us.

Knowing that doesn't always soothe the heart. The heart ignores logic. The heart replays the what-ifs, the maybes, the if-onlys. Nothing but the full, unshakable truth can silence them.

When so much around his death remains blurred, tangled, unresolved — those questions only echo louder.
And make it that much harder to understand.

In the months that followed, I often wondered if I would ever forgive myself — not because I had done something wrong, but because I had done something human. Because I had tried, and fought, and loved, and reached the end of what I could hold and endure.

This is the quiet shadow I still carry. Not only the loss of my husband, but the loss of the man I was fighting so hard to save. The loss of the marriage I still believed could be repaired. The loss of the future I was still hoping to salvage, even as everything was falling apart.

Tough love is called tough for a reason.

And sometimes, it's not the love itself that breaks you— it's the questions it leaves behind. The *what-ifs*, the *should I have*, the *was that the moment*...Questions that become the heaviest weight of all.

People avoid talking about it. Tough love doesn't always lead to healing or growth. Sometimes, it backfires. Sometimes, it turns ugly. It doesn't result in what we hoped for — or even what we expected.

We set boundaries, believing they'll lead to clarity.

We step back, thinking it might bring them closer.

Sometimes, all it creates is distance. Silence.

Sometimes…it becomes the last chapter, not the turning point. Not the *happily ever after* we so fiercely hoped for.

Not the ending we fought for, prayed for, held on so tightly to.

The Nature of Grief

Grief has no boundaries. No rules. No neat conclusion, script, or timeline society approves.

It doesn't matter if you're at work, in the grocery store, or smiling at a photo. It hits when it wants — loud, raw, and unforgiving.

People expect it to fade.

To get easier.

To be wrapped up and tucked away like a chapter you've finished reading.

Grief isn't linear. It loops. It lingers. And sometimes, it doesn't merely visit — it becomes a permanent presence.

It slips past walls you thought were strong, bypasses every defense you carefully built. It does not care how old you are, how strong you are, how much you pray or beg or distract yourself.

It does not discriminate.

It arrives raw, relentless — and it tears you open.

Grief is the great uninvited guest that takes up residence in your chest, in your bones, in the hollow spaces behind your ribs. It can't be hidden from. It can't be outrun.

Even when you think you've managed to tuck it neatly away, sealed up tight inside some hidden corner of your heart, it finds its way back. And when it returns, it comes harder, louder, breaking through the surface when you least expect it — in a song on the radio, in the smell of his cologne on an old jacket, in the taste of a meal you haven't made in years, in the way your hand still reaches for someone who is no longer there.

They say time will heal.

I call bullshit.

Here's the truth no one tells you: There are still times, even now, twelve years later, when one of those stages of grief rises again.

Time doesn't heal. Time distracts. Time teaches you how to carry it differently. Time helps you build a life around the crater that grief leaves behind. But grief itself? It never fully heals.

It gets softer, yes. It gets quieter, retreating into the deeper layers of your soul where it can rest for a while. You can go days, weeks, sometimes even months without feeling it flood your chest. Nevertheless — it never truly leaves.

It lingers, like an echo you've learned to live with. It moves to the back, it tucks itself into the corners, it lets you breathe more freely — but it never dies. It becomes part of you — not as a wound to be erased, but as a scar you carry forward, proof that you loved, proof that you lost, proof that you survived.

IT never dies.

Who Was I Now?

The question played in my head constantly. I remember sitting alone on the couch, staring at the TV — half-watching it. Not crying, not screaming — empty. Numb.

Asking myself, over and over:

Who am I now?

What am I supposed to do with this life, now that everything I built it around is gone?

I wasn't just grieving him. I was grieving who I had been. I was grieving the woman who had been a wife, a mother in a full house, a co-builder of dreams.

58

The person who cared for a house of children, ran to practices, cooked dinners. The wife who built her life around her husband's drinking and bipolar episodes — always managing, always smoothing things over, always holding it together.

That woman didn't exist anymore.

Those roles didn't exist anymore.

I didn't know how to be anything else.

I hadn't realized until then, after twenty-five years, that I had lost my own identity. I had wrapped my whole life around them. I truly didn't know what I liked to do. I didn't know what foods I cared for myself. I didn't know what dreams I had for me.

I had only Jan and Van as true friends. I never let anyone else get close.

It was an epiphany that was hard to swallow.

How did I get here?

How had I let this happen?

What Stayed with Me

Even now, when I think back on that time, I don't remember the days or the dates. I remember the heavy stillness of the house. I remember the paperwork. I remember the ache in my body that wouldn't go away. I remember the feeling of sitting in a car packed with the last of my things, pulling away from the driveway, thinking:

What else can God take from me? I miscarried a child. I gave a husband. Why do I have to give everything else — our home, our dreams, our future? What have I done so wrong in life?

That question still lingers.

No one tells you how it sticks. How it becomes part of the fabric of your thoughts. Not loud all the time, but ever-present. Sometimes quiet, sometimes screaming. Always there.

It becomes the shadow that walks beside you. Not stopping you — but shaping you.

Tainting joy. Coloring hope.

A reminder that the rug can be ripped out at any moment. That love doesn't always get a happy ending. That survival sometimes means letting go of everything you once clung to.

What stayed with me wasn't only the pain of losing him. It was the silence after. The unanswered questions. The weight of starting over without the person I built everything with.

It was the slow, painful work of trying to rebuild a life from the wreckage of one that didn't get to finish.

Chapter Five:
As the Dust Settles

"Survival isn't the absence of breaking —
it's the quiet,
trembling choice to keep rising after you've shattered."

The Lingering Weight

When the funerals are over and the world quiets down, one might think the hardest part is behind you. The calls slowed. The sympathy cards stopped arriving. The casseroles stopped appearing at the door. People went back to their lives, their routines, their own orbit.

But for us, the hardest part wasn't over.

It had only started.

Because grief doesn't end when the ceremonies do. It lingers, heavy and unspoken, inside the same house, the same walls, the same rooms — the same air where his absence echoed.

I stayed in that house for only fifteen more months after his death. Fifteen months of trying to hold everything together. Fifteen months of waking up every morning, putting both feet on the floor, and telling myself, *Get up. Keep going. Your son needs you.* Fifteen months of being both mom and dad to my youngest son, who was only nine — a boy too young to fully understand the weight of death, but old enough to feel the void it left.

There was no family nearby.

No one to lean on.

No grandparents to swoop in and help with school pickup.

No siblings to stop by and check on us.

No one to fill the aching, invisible space where a father used to stand.

It was me and my son.

Two hearts, both broken in different ways, trying to find a rhythm that didn't feel like survival. But most days, it was survival.

I worked full-time. I kept the house running — the bills paid, the groceries bought, the laundry folded. I made sure my son got to school, to football practice, to every little thing that might remind him that life still had shape, still had motion, still had some kind of normalcy — even when nothing in our world was normal anymore.

Behind closed doors, there were nights when I cried alone in the kitchen after he went to bed. When the weight of *being everything* pressed so hard on my chest, I wondered if I would break. I didn't. Because I couldn't.

Every morning, I showed up.

Not perfectly.

Not gracefully.

But fully, fiercely, determined.

I tried, every day, to hold both of us up. To be the scaffolding when the walls of our world had cracked. To be the soft place for my son's grief to land, even when I didn't know where to put my own. To keep the lights on, the lunches packed, the schedules moving — to make sure he had not just survival, but some thread of joy, some thread of connection, some reminder that he was still loved, still safe, still held.

What no one tells you is that after the dust settles, grief doesn't pack its bags and leave. It moves in. It becomes the quiet third presence in the house — sitting at the dinner table, echoing in the empty chair, brushing past you in the hallways at night.

So, you do what you can.

You carry it.

You lift yourself up and, in doing so, lift the ones you love.

Even when you're tired.

Even when you're lonely.

Even when you wonder if anyone sees how hard you're trying. If anyone even cares.

The Hardest Hours

The days were hard — but the nights were worse.

During the day, I could survive by staying in motion. Work. Errands. Appointments. Practices. My son gave me structure, and routine became my lifeline. There was always something to do — someone to call, an activity to attend, a meal to prepare, a bill to pay.

If I kept moving, I didn't have to feel it all. If I stayed busy, the grief waited at the edges, lingering in the periphery of my perception. So, I stayed busy. Bringing work home to keep the mind active and engaged. Practice and scouts to keep out of an empty house. Digging into researching the afterlife and what else might be out there. What was the church not wanting us to find out? What they didn't want to teach.

In the dark of night, everything stopped. The house grew quiet. The dishes were done. The lights were dim. The child was asleep.

At that point, I found myself alone.

Me and the walls.

Me and the silence.

Me and the endless echo of memories I couldn't stop.

In the stillness, the mind wandered — not gently, not peacefully — but restlessly, painfully, compulsively. A hundred unanswered questions swirled through my head like a storm. *What if I had been there sooner? What if I had noticed something was wrong? What if I had said one more thing, done one more thing, held on tighter, stayed up later?*

The *why* circled like a predator — unanswerable, insatiable, gnawing at my heart. Why him? Why now? Why like this?

But the questions that haunted me weren't solely about his death — they were about my part in the story. The divorce papers had been my last attempt at tough love, filed not to end us, but to shake him into seeking help. To choose us over himself. Yet, they were in the mailbox the day he died. Did he see them? Was it too hard? Did I push too far? That ache, that uncertainty, became a grief all its own, woven into every decision I would make from that point forward.

At night, the mask came off. I could finally let the tears fall without worrying who might see. No one would be made uncomfortable by my sobbing. No one would offer words they didn't know how to give. I didn't have to explain or hold it in. I could collapse, unseen. I could unravel, unnoticed.

But that kind of solitude was both a relief and a cruelty. Because when the panic hit — and it often did — there was no one there. There were so many nights when I woke up gasping, heart hammering in my chest, the sheets tangled around my legs, the dark room feeling too small, too cold, too empty. So scared I could not move; the dreams so lifelike and vivid that I half expected to open my eyes and still find myself trapped inside them. My body would be frozen, caught somewhere between sleep and waking, my breath shallow and quick, every shadow in the room twisting into something dangerous.

Minutes felt like hours before I could force myself to merely move a hand, to whisper into the silence to remind myself I was still here. Even then, the fear clung to me, a residue that didn't fade with daylight.

I reached across the bed out of instinct, half-asleep, hoping to feel the weight of him next to me — but my hand touched nothing but cold blankets and an emptiness so sharp it cut.

I wanted arms to pull me close.

I wanted a voice to whisper *It's okay.*

I wanted to be held until I could steady my own breath.

But there was only silence. Over and over. Me, alone, wrapped in a grief so loud it filled every corner of the room.

There were nights when the clock seemed to mock me. 2 a.m. 3:30 a.m. 5:15 a.m. Each hour passed, not with the softness of sleep, but with the weight of survival — minute by minute, heartbeat by heartbeat — wishing grief would allow me this one grace: peaceful sleep. But it never did.

Instead, it kept me suspended in that shadowy space between exhaustion and dread, where rest was always out of reach and the night stretched on like a sentence with no end. I wondered if the sun would ever rise again. If I would ever rise again.

The hardest hours weren't measured by the clock. They were measured by absence. By the cold side of the bed. By the empty air where laughter used to live. By the ache in my chest that no one could see, but that felt like it would split me open.

These were the hours when I realized how fragile I was. How human. How breakable. Yet — these were also the hours when, somehow, I kept breathing. When my body, despite everything, kept pulling in air, kept forcing blood through my veins, kept whispering *not yet, not yet — stay.*

I didn't know it then, but those were the nights I was learning the shape of my own endurance.

Not strength that looked like triumph.

Not strength that looked like victory.

But strength that looked like *staying.*

Strength that looked like making it to morning, even when I didn't know how.

Small Cracks of Light

Laughter returned — quietly at first, like a shy visitor at the door, hesitant to come in.

Smiles began to creep back onto our faces, though sometimes they surprised me when they arrived, like: *Oh... there you are. I remember you.*

It became easier — or at least less impossible — to get out of bed each morning. Let's be honest: I didn't get up for myself. I got up because of my son.

He needed me more than ever.

In the aftermath of everything, when the world had been reduced to ash and unanswered questions, he became my lifeline — even though I was supposed to be his. He gave me purpose when I felt like I had none. He gave me structure when my days threatened to dissolve into grief and numbness. He was the reason I planted my feet on the floor each day, no matter how heavy they felt.

We found small anchors; little pockets of normalcy we could wrap our hands around.

Football.

Scouts.

Weekend games. Boy Scout meetings.

These became more than activities — they became our lifelines. They gave my son a place to laugh again, to be a child, to run wild with his friends and feel, for a few precious hours, like life hadn't fallen apart. They gave him something to look forward to — something that wasn't shrouded in grief or whispered condolences.

And for me?

For me, they were a beautiful distraction, too. For those moments, I wasn't the widow. I wasn't the woman who had lost her husband, her dreams, her home. I was just a mom on the sidelines — clapping, cheering, passing out snacks, tying shoelaces, laughing with the other parents.

There, in those small, ordinary moments, we weren't "the family who had lost everything." We were simply a mom and a son — cheering together, leaning on each other, sharing tiny bursts of joy inside the storm.

I started to realize that healing didn't arrive as one big, dramatic wave crashing in to wash the pain away.

It arrived in small cracks of light.

In a giggle over spilled popcorn at the game. In a high-five on the sidelines after a touchdown. In the warm, tired hug at the end of the day when we both collapsed onto the couch.

It wasn't the life we had planned.

It wasn't the life we had dreamed.

Inside the ruins, we were beginning — slowly, quietly — to rebuild something new.

Not because the grief was gone. Not because the pain had disappeared. But because, even in the heaviest darkness, light always finds its way through.

A Silent Shift in Faith

In that time — that long, strange time after death knocked at my door — I wasn't sure where my faith stood.

I wanted so badly to believe that God was still near, still watching, still holding me. Some days, it felt as if He had quietly turned His back. Like I was calling out into an empty canyon, my voice ricocheting off stone, coming back to me unanswered.

I felt abandoned — by the people who should have stood by, God Himself, and the church that had once shaped the bones of my life.

Some nights, I folded my hands and prayed the way I always had, whispering words I had learned as a child. Other nights, I sat there in silence, staring into the dim corners of my room, wondering if anyone — or anything — was even listening at all.

Here's the raw truth I didn't dare say aloud: the praying didn't help.

The prayers I had whispered for years, the ones I had offered faithfully, the ones I clung to like lifelines — none of them had been answered. Not in the way I had hoped. Not in the moments I needed most. Now, when the stakes were higher than they had ever been, when I was pleading for answers about the unsolved death of my husband — I was met with nothing but silence.

Crickets.

God had taken my husband.

Taken my dreams.

Left me empty-handed, hollowed out, staring at a life that had been reduced to ashes.

And to top it off, there was no explanation.

No why.

No how.

No by whom.

I pleaded over and over again in prayer: Why?

Why did this happen?

How could this happen?

Who was responsible?

And when no answer came, when the heavens stayed sealed shut, I began to wonder: How does a person keep faith in a God who does not answer? How do you continue to believe in a merciful God when mercy seems so glaringly absent?

I realized something I hadn't been able to articulate before: living within religious indoctrination — the rules, the rituals, the outward symbols — was not the same as living by values.

My values — the deep moral compass that guided how I treated people, how I loved, how I gave — had been shaped by religion, yes. But my belief in the religious structures? That was something else entirely.

Slowly, quietly, imperceptibly at first, my faith began to shift.

It didn't happen in one angry moment, or one dramatic declaration of disbelief. It was a silent evolution, like the slow turning of the tide, the quiet bending of a branch under the weight of accumulated snow.

I found myself pulled away from the hard-edged doctrines I had once accepted without questioning and toward something else. Toward something softer. Something more spiritual. Something more expansive.

It was not a rejection of faith, but a reshaping.

I didn't have a name for it yet. I couldn't define it or explain it. Deep down, I could feel it: something inside me was beginning to stir — quietly, gently, in the places where the old faith had cracked and let light through.

A new kind of faith was being born, not in the sanctuaries or sermons, but in the raw, aching spaces of grief where all the old answers had fallen away.

The Moment That Pierced Through

Then, one night — a handful of months after the funeral, after the endless paperwork, after the long, quiet nights — my son looked at me with those honest, searching eyes and said, *"Mom... I need a dad."*

It was like a knife straight to the chest, but sharper than grief, because it cut through layers I thought I had protected. I hadn't seen it coming. I hadn't prepared for that sentence, that truth, spoken so simply, so vulnerably, by a child who had lost as much as I had. The room seemed to still, as if even the air knew this was a moment that would mark me forever.

I froze in shock. My heart squeezed, and the grief surged fresh, but this time it wasn't only my own. It was his too. His longing. His need. His words told me more than he could have possibly known — that while I was lost in the wreckage of my own pain, he was navigating an emptiness of his own, one I could never fully fill.

He needs a dad.

He wants a dad.

Beneath that truth was an unspoken plea: *Will you help me find the part of my life that feels missing?*

In that moment, I realized what it meant — what it asked of me. It meant I would have to start thinking about dating again. Not someday, not in a distant and untouchable future I could keep postponing. Now. It wasn't just about me anymore. My choices, my hesitations, my fear — they were no longer mine alone to carry.

Was I ready? Could I open myself up when my heart still felt like a pile of broken glass, each piece sharp enough to cut anyone who got too close? Could I risk it — the vulnerability, the awkwardness, the fear — when every part of me still felt raw and bruised? Did I even want to?

Grief had taught me to guard my world, to keep the walls high and the gates locked. But his words pressed against those walls, not in anger, in longing. And that longing cracked something open in me.

Carefully, cautiously, I began. Slowly, quietly, privately. No one came to the house. No one met my son. Not unless they were *the* man — the right man, the one who would accept not only me but *us*, no questions asked, no conditions attached.

Unexpectedly — almost as if life had been holding him back until I was ready — I met him. The man who would become the next chapter in our story.

Promise to Ourselves

When he said those words — *"Mom... I need a dad"* — something deep inside me cracked open. It wasn't merely grief shifting; it was responsibility reshaping itself inside me. I felt it settle in my bones: the weight of us.

I promised myself I would hold us together — even if it meant losing pieces of myself along the way. Even if it meant folding my own dreams into corners, tucking away the parts of me that once longed for freedom, spontaneity, or simply a moment to breathe.

I would carry the weight of us, both of us, on these shoulders, because the bond between a mother and her child was one I refused to let fracture — no matter how heavy it became.

I would carry us forward, even when the road ahead was foggy, uncertain, and steep. Even without a map, without guideposts, without guarantees. Even when I was terrified, when every step felt like a gamble, when the future looked like a question mark wrapped in storm clouds. I would keep walking, keep choosing the next right thing, keep reaching for light — because standing still wasn't an option when little eyes were watching and little hands were trusting me to lead.

Chapter Six:
God's Silence

"When heaven locked its doors, I stopped knocking —
and learned to roar my own prayers."

Spiritual Void

When the noise finally faded and the house grew quiet, I found myself facing not only grief, but something even deeper, even more unsettling:

Where was God in all of this?

I knew the prayers — the familiar cadence of Hail Mary, Our Father, Glory Be. I knew the rituals — crossing myself at the holy water font, kneeling in the pew, lighting candles for intentions.

I knew the sacraments — baptism, confirmation, communion, confession, marriage. I knew the seasons — Advent, Lent, Easter, Christmas. I knew how to sit in the sanctuary, how to fold my hands, how to bow my head, how to whisper words of faith.

For most of my life, I believed — or at least, I wanted to believe — that God was near. That He was listening. That He was present. That even in the darkest hours, He would not leave me alone.

When my husband died, a part of me shifted in ways I couldn't name

The prayers I had whispered for years seemed to vanish before they reached heaven, dissolving into the air like they had nowhere to land.

The rituals felt empty in my hands — mechanical, rehearsed, as if I were reciting lines from someone else's script. The sanctuary, once my refuge, now felt cold and unwelcoming, its walls strangers to me. The God I had been taught to trust felt silent — distant — or worse, unmoved. Stepping into the church no longer brought peace; it brought a hollow ache. The thread that had once tethered me there had snapped, and I could feel the fray.

I remember sitting in the pews in those first months after the funeral, hearing the soft murmur of prayers, the readings of scripture, and wondering if anyone around me knew I was barely holding on. Did they know I was drowning beneath the surface, gasping for air? Did they know I had questions burning inside me, questions I was too afraid to say out loud?

Why, God?

Why did You let this happen?

Why did You take him?

Why did You leave me here, in this emptiness, in this loneliness, with so many unanswered questions?

I wasn't just grieving a man, a marriage, a life — I was grieving a God I no longer recognized.

A God who had been my anchor, my compass, my hope — and now felt like a stranger.

I had been faithful.

I stayed through the hard years, through the sickness, through the drinking, through the fights, through the chaos. I had honored my vows — for better or worse, in sickness and in health, 'til death do us part. And when death came, I expected God to catch me. To hold me. To at least meet me in the pain.

Instead, all I met was silence.

Not a soft, comforting silence — but an echoing, roaring, crushing silence, like standing in a canyon and shouting out my pain, only to hear it bounce back at me unanswered.

Where was God in all of this? Why did He turn away when I needed Him most? And if He hadn't turned away, why couldn't I feel Him? Why couldn't I hear Him? Why did He let me shatter like this, without sending even a whisper of comfort?

This wasn't just a spiritual crisis — it was a breaking of everything I thought I knew, a crumbling of the scaffolding I had built my life upon.

Yet, even in the hollow of that silence, something in me — a flicker, a breath, a whisper — wondered: If God wasn't in the place I had always been told to look for Him… was He somewhere else? And if He was… how would I find Him again?

The Silence That Roared

At first, I prayed like I always had. The way I was taught throughout school. Lying awake at night, hands folded, eyes squeezed shut, I whispered desperate, aching prayers:

Why?

How?

Who?

I prayed for answers — not for comfort, but for clarity. Why did this happen? How could this have happened? Who was responsible?

I begged for something concrete, something to hold onto. The case remained unsolved. The circumstances remained murky. In the fog, I reached up toward heaven and the God I was taught to believe in.

When no answers came — when the heavens stayed closed, when my prayers seemed to dissolve into the walls, when all I received was a relentless, aching silence — something inside me began to fracture.

I was carrying more than grief. It was betrayal. It was abandonment. It was the piercing realization that the God I had believed in — the merciful God, the protective God, the ever-present God — had turned His face away. Not only through silence, but through the actions of the very churches that claimed to speak for Him.

I looked around at my shattered life and wondered: Where was that mercy I had been promised? Where was that divine protection I had prayed for all those years? Where was the guiding hand I had clung to through every storm, only to now be left standing, wrecked and alone?

There were days — and many, many nights — when I raged at God. I thundered in fury.

In raw, searing heartbreak. In disbelief that after everything I had endured — the fights, the years of dysfunction, the trauma, the heartbreak, the efforts to hold it all together — this was how it ended.

I had spent years on my knees, begging Him to intervene. To let my husband change. To help our family heal. To bring peace where there was chaos. To soften the blows. To give us one more chance. To let the final act of tough love work.

Instead, He let it all collapse. He let me become the woman left behind — the woman raising a child alone, the woman picking up the shards of a life she had poured everything into, the woman sitting inside a house that no longer felt like home, the woman staring into an emptiness she had never imagined.

My rage was not only at God's silence, but at feeling He had broken the hope I'd held for years. Hope that my prayers mattered. Hope that my faith counted for something. Hope that if I held on tight enough, prayed hard enough, things would turn around.

I begged, I pleaded, I sobbed for clarity: Was this homicide? Was it suicide? Was it something I could have stopped? Was there something I missed? Please tell me, God — give me an answer, so I could have closure, so I could stop living in the suffocating limbo of what-ifs and maybes.

All I met was silence. And with that silence came more questions. And with those questions came more rage. The silence didn't calm me. It ignited me. It fueled a fire in my chest that burned hotter the longer I waited for a divine response that never came.

This wasn't the comforting, peaceful faith I had been raised on. This was standing in the ruins of belief, shouting into a void, and realizing no one was answering back.

When Compassion and Security Collapse

Here's the brutal truth I learned in the months after his death:

Loss doesn't merely take the person you love. It takes your sense of safety. It takes your sense of belonging. And sometimes, it takes the very compassion you thought would be there to catch you.

I felt the absence of compassion everywhere I turned.

The priest who refused to perform the funeral because of religious rules — no comfort, no embrace, no offer of mercy, simply cold, bureaucratic "no," as if I was just another woman off the street, not a wife, not a grieving widow, not a soul on the edge of collapse.

The cemetery that resisted letting his body be placed in the family plot — no compassion for the man's life, for his roots, for the heartbreak left behind, only rules and refusals and technicalities.

The church that was supposed to hold me in my sorrow, that was supposed to walk beside me in my time of need — it turned away. It shut its doors. It said, in so many silent ways: You are not one of us anymore.

The most painful loss of all: the security I had once believed came from religious belonging. That security had been built into me from childhood — the idea that no matter how bad things got, the church would be my safe place. The place where I could kneel down and cry, where I could light a candle and feel a flicker of hope, where someone — anyone — would put a hand on my shoulder and remind me I wasn't alone.

I had been taught that the church was my spiritual family. That the faith community was a net ready to catch me when I fell. That the rituals, the prayers, the sacraments were scaffolding meant to hold me steady when everything else crumbled. I believed in that security with the unshakable faith of a child who had never been shown otherwise.

In the moment of my greatest need, when I reached out for that lifeline, it was not there. The security I had trusted so fully shattered like glass in my hands. I realized that what I thought had been a foundation was, in fact, conditional — offered only when you fit inside the lines, when you followed the rules, when you didn't challenge or disrupt or fall apart too loudly.

It wasn't that compassion was withheld. It was that the very structure I had leaned on for strength — faith, ritual, community, belief — cracked and crumbled, leaving me exposed, unanchored, uncertain.

Where was the compassion I had been taught to believe in? Where was the mercy I was told God offers to the brokenhearted? Where was the soft landing I thought faith was supposed to provide?

It wasn't just the loss of my husband. It was the loss of trust, of faith, of the belief that the religious dogma I had lived under was there to uphold me in crisis. Compassion and security, the two pillars I had leaned on, fell away — and I was left standing in the rubble, wondering if they had ever truly been real.

Going Through the Motions

On the outside, I kept up appearances. We still went to church. My son still attended religion classes. We celebrated Christmas, Advent, Lent. We spoke God's name. To the outside world, it looked like we were holding steady, like our faith was intact. However inside? Inside, I was crumbling.

I didn't realize it at the time, I stayed in the pews not for myself, but for my son — to give him the stability, the routine, the foundation I no longer felt for myself. I wanted him to have something to stand on, even as the ground beneath my own feet gave way. I wanted him to have an anchor, a framework of belief, even if I was no longer sure I believed myself.

For me, it was hollow.

Every sermon became harder and harder to sit through. I sat there, listening as they preached: Love all. Help thy neighbor. Turn the other cheek. Tithe to the church. Trust in God's mercy. All I could think was: Where was God when I needed Him? Where was the church when I asked for help? Where was the compassion I was taught to model, the mercy I was told to trust?

I remembered the priest who refused to perform my husband's funeral. The cemetery that wouldn't take his body because of rules and paperwork. The very people and institutions who should have wrapped me in comfort, who should have held me as I fell apart — they had turned away, closed their doors, closed their hearts.

And that's when I realized something deep, something unsettling: Living within religious indoctrination is not the same as living by values.

My values — compassion, love, integrity, generosity — those remained. They were woven into my bones, shaped by my upbringing, shaped by my experience. They were how I lived my life, how I raised my children, how I moved through the world.

My belief in the religious structures, the doctrines, the rules? That began to slip away.

Confession.

Tithing.

The idea that our pain and suffering had a divine purpose.

The idea that if you were faithful, God would protect you.

All of it started to feel less like truth and more like control. I found myself stepping back — not only with anger, but with quiet disillusionment. I was still standing in the sanctuary. My heart was no longer there.

If I was honest with myself, maybe it never fully had been.

Even as a child, I remember questioning. I remember the priest saying we were not to reach out to the dead, that they had their tasks in the afterlife, that they couldn't be bothered by us. Even then, something inside me stirred, whispering: Why? That doesn't make sense. Why would a loving God seal off love? Why would connection end because a heartbeat stopped?

Now, as an adult facing loss and betrayal, those childhood whispers returned — but they were no longer whispers. They were loud, insistent, undeniable. They echoed in my mind as I sat through sermons I no longer believed, rituals that no longer touched me, prayers that no longer stirred anything inside. I was going through the motions, yes — but the motions no longer moved me.

Quietly, without fanfare or announcement, something inside me began to shift. Not a rejection. Not yet. A deep, restless questioning. A knowing that whatever came next, whatever faith I was destined to rebuild, it would have to be on my own terms — shaped not by rules or guilt or obligation, but by the raw, fierce truths I was beginning to uncover inside myself.

The Quiet Beginning of Something Else

I didn't walk away from God overnight. There was no dramatic moment where I slammed a Bible shut, no fiery rejection, no shouting at the heavens that I was done. It was slower than that. Quieter. Like a tide pulling back from the shore, like snow sliding off a branch under its own quiet weight. It was the slow, aching undoing of something I had once believed would hold me forever — a gentle erosion of trust, not a thunderous collapse.

What surprised me most was not the crumbling of old faith, but the tender stirrings that emerged in its absence. As my old faith began to slip through the cracks, something else began to stir. I didn't have words for it yet. I couldn't have named it or pointed to it or even prayed toward it. I felt it: a quiet longing, a subtle curiosity, a pull toward something softer, something more expansive, something beyond the strict lines of religious doctrine. Something outside organized religion.

I began to notice how the God I had been taught to fear no longer fit the shape of my pain or my questions. The sermons no longer answered the ache in my chest. The rituals no longer soothed the confusion in my heart. Yet, in that empty space, I could feel something shimmering beyond reach — a possibility, a hint, a whisper of another way to believe.

It wasn't anger that moved me forward. It wasn't rebellion or rejection. It was something gentler, something more essential: the quiet instinct that told me, even when faith crumbled, even when the old words no longer held, there was still something sacred waiting to be found. A presence not confined to pews or altars or doctrines. A Divine who could

85

meet me in the rawness of my grief, in the silent ache of my questions, in the simple, everyday moments when I had nothing left but breath and hope.

Looking Ahead

I didn't know it then, but I was standing on the edge of a spiritual evolution. Moving from the God of the church to the Divine of the universe. From doctrine to mystery. From rigid rules to a living, breathing relationship. But before I could step fully into that space, I had to walk through the shadowed rooms of loss, anger, betrayal, and silence. I had to let myself crumble so that something new could eventually rise.

So, Chapter Six closes not with resolution, not with triumph, but with a woman standing alone in the quiet, her heart still heavy with grief, her faith threadbare and trembling, wondering if God is still there — and beginning, just beginning, to imagine that maybe, just maybe, faith is bigger, wilder, and more beautiful than she was ever taught to believe.

Chapter Seven:
The Shift from God to Creator, Universe, Mother/Father Divine

*"I unstitched the fabric of old prayers
and found the stars sewn quietly into my own skin."*

Peeling the Layers

Before I could face the deepest shadows inside myself, I had to step back and examine the spiritual framework that had shaped me.

I had to ask hard, intimate questions: Who or what is God to me now? What am I anchored to when the doctrines fall away? Where do I find meaning when the rituals no longer soothe the ache?

I had to confront not only the loss of old religious structures but also the raw uncertainty of carving out a faith that belonged solely to me — without a guidebook, without a map, without anyone else's permission.

It required peeling back layers of indoctrination, fear, and guilt, and allowing myself to feel the terrifying freedom of listening inward instead of outward.

This process wasn't neat or linear. It was messy, vulnerable, and deeply emotional — a gradual shedding of borrowed beliefs so I could make space for a spirituality molded by my own lived experience, my own grief, my own healing, and my own wild, evolving connection to the Divine.

This wasn't only about questioning my beliefs — it was about opening a door to something bigger, something wilder, something more intimate and alive than anything I had ever been taught. It was about stepping beyond religious indoctrination and into a living, breathing relationship with the Divine — one shaped not by external rules, but by inner resonance, intuition, personal experience, and deep emotional connection.

I began to feel the Divine not as a distant authority, but as a Presence woven through my grief, my joy, my healing, and my moments of quiet surrender.

It became a spirituality that molded me in new ways: teaching me to trust my own wisdom, to honor the sacredness of my questions, and to rest in the unfolding mystery rather than fear it.

This shift was not a change in belief; it was a profound reshaping of how I moved through the world — more open, more tender, more aligned with the pulsing, breathing truth of the Divine within and around me. Flowing in the very essence of creation.

It was here, in this reimagining of God, that my real spiritual journey began.

Where the Shift Began

Looking back, the shift wasn't instant. It wasn't a sudden rejection of everything I had been taught — it was the slow, quiet unraveling of a belief system that no longer fit the woman I was becoming.

It started subtly, almost innocently. In college, I signed up for a course on death and dying. I expected it to be academic, maybe even clinical, but instead, it cracked open something inside me. We pulled back the curtain on one of life's most mysterious and avoided subjects. *What happens after we die? What do other cultures believe? How do we face mortality with grace, purpose, and meaning?*

For the first time, I felt permission — not from the church, but from within myself — to sit with these questions without rushing to tidy them up with an answer. The conversations in that class fascinated me. They held an honesty I had never heard in Sunday sermons, an acknowledgment of mystery instead of a formula for certainty. It was as if someone had slid open a window in a room I didn't realize was suffocating me.

I wasn't drawn to the fear of death, as the church had taught me to be. I was drawn to the awe of it. To the mystery. To the quiet invitation to explore something bigger, something deeper, something more expansive than the narrow narratives I'd been given.

But with curiosity came tension.

This new way of seeing the world only left me with more questions, and questioning the church was not allowed. I was taught to abide by its rules, to silence anything that didn't fit neatly into its doctrines. So, I kept my questions to myself — hidden like contraband, tucked away where no one could accuse me of rebellion.

Yet even in silence, the questions refused to die. They pulsed quietly in the background of my life, shaping my thoughts, coloring my prayers, tugging at the edges of my faith. The pull toward something I couldn't name — something I couldn't fully understand — never left. And in time, I would come to see that it was not a threat to my faith at all, but the beginning of its transformation.

The Psychic Doorway

After my mother passed in 2002, that door squeaked open. I remember sitting alone late at night, consumed by grief but also consumed by an aching curiosity: where did she go? Could she hear me? I began diving into books like Sylvia Browne's *Life on the Other Side: A Psychic's Tour of the Afterlife*. It wasn't just an intellectual fascination — it was a lifeline.

I was drawn to these pages like a thirsty woman stumbling upon water, desperate for answers, for connection, for hope that the bonds of love didn't simply end with death. It opened possibilities I only considered in passing — that maybe, just maybe, we could communicate with those who had crossed over. That maybe the soul continues on, reachable not through priests or church rituals, but through something more personal, more intuitive, more mystical. Maybe, one day, I could speak to Mom myself. Cross those boundaries we don't speak of — and reclaim a connection I wasn't ready to surrender. You weren't supposed to think that way as a good catholic.

When my husband died, it was no surprise that I was catapulted back into that world. I needed to understand what truly happens when we die. I wanted answers to the questions the church either couldn't — or wouldn't — answer. The mysteries they sidestepped, wrapped in doctrine, as if the truth was too dangerous, too uncontainable, for ordinary people to know.

Three weeks after his death, I sought out a local psychic — hoping for answers, hoping to know he had crossed over. That he was in the heaven I had been taught about all my life. That even if his death was by suicide, he was allowed to enter. I needed to know where he was, if he was safe, if he still existed somewhere beyond my reach. Maybe, just maybe, get the answer to why.

Sharlette couldn't give me the reason I was desperate for— the *why* that haunted every waking moment—but she did offer something else: the comfort of knowing he had crossed. She told me he had been waiting, lingering between worlds, until the day I came to see her. That my visit had been the moment he was waiting for, the doorway he needed to finally step through. The thought that he had held on for me—waiting for our connection one last time before moving on—was both a balm and a heartbreak I didn't know how to hold.

A couple weeks later, my daughter and I attended a local psychic fair hosted by Shatlette. The church had always warned against such things, but I was pulled there anyway, craving connection, craving answers the church had not provided. Looking for the answers the investigation wasn't providing. Why? Who?

It was there I met Peggy, a channeler of the angelic realm and energy practitioner. With skepticism, I sat for an oracle card reading that day. I told her nothing while my daughter and I sat there — silent, nervous, almost holding our breath. We listened as she turned each card and delivered messages. Each one resonated, striking chords deep inside me I hadn't even known were waiting.

It was the last card she turned over that fractured something in me. Tears came fast, catching me off guard. I smiled through them, swept under by a wave of recognition, awe, and an almost unfamiliar relief. I didn't understand what was happening or how — but I felt it all the same.

A simple, small image on the card — a red heart with wings flying — gave me all the proof I needed. Peggy looked at us, eyes soft, as we cried and stared, unable to speak.

A couple weeks earlier, I had gotten a tattoo on my shoulder in remembrance of my husband: a heart filled with the American flag design with wings flying. Almost an identical image that represented him.

How? How could that be? Out of seventy-two cards, what were the odds would it be that one?

Seeing that card wasn't coincidence. It was a message, a sign, the thread of connection I had been desperate for. I needed no more proof—he was on the other side, reaching for me. In the months that followed, every time Peggy did a reading, that card appeared again—each time, a quiet, astonishing reminder that he was still near, watching over us, loving us from beyond the veil.

Peggy became a mentor, friend, and mother figure —
someone who stepped into my life at a time when I was raw
with grief and desperate for something, anything, to help me
breathe again.

She guided me through the bewildering emotional
landscape I was facing, opening the door even wider to the
"other side" — to the possibility that death was not the end,
that love still flowed between worlds. At the heart of it, I
learned that communication between worlds was not only
possible — it was not a sin, and it was nothing to fear.

Peggy introduced me to books like *When God Pinched My Toe*
by Dr. Kathryn E. May, a collection of channeled messages
from divine sources—Mother/Father God, Ascended Masters,
and other beings of higher consciousness. She sent me
Facebook pages, forwarded emails, and shared anything she
thought might help me navigate this new way of thinking. More
than handing me books, she became a living bridge — showing
me, by example, what it meant to walk in two worlds: the
visible and the invisible, the human and the divine.

She understood my spiritual condition. She, too, had been
raised Catholic her whole life, steeped in tradition, ritual, and
the unspoken boundaries of what could and couldn't be
questioned. She, too, had felt the quiet pull of something
greater—an internal beacon that refused to be silenced, even
when it led her beyond the walls of the church. She knew what
it was to wrestle with doubt and wonder in equal measure, to
follow a thread of truth into unfamiliar territory, trusting it
would lead somewhere sacred.

Our conversations were endless, each one a lifeline, each
one unlocking new insights and deeper questions. I couldn't
absorb the information fast enough — I was hungry for it,
thirsty for it, aching for it. It struck me so deeply, I felt it in

every fiber of my being. It felt like truth. It felt like home. It felt like I was finally remembering something I had always known but had been taught to forget.

Learning that Jesus may have had a wife and family, that there were angels and Ascended Masters surrounding us, ready to assist when asked — these were revelations that reshaped my worldview.

That same spiritual power and divine presence weren't reserved for clergy or mystics — they lived within each of us. You didn't have to be special to reach them.

I discovered that we are here for our souls to grow, that every trial and tribulation is an opportunity to move closer to the Creator.

With profound impact, I realized we can speak directly to our loved ones beyond the veil — that death does not sever the bond, only changes its form.

This knowledge didn't just challenge my old religious framework; it smashed it wide open. I began to see how the organized religion I had once clung to had used fear to control me, to keep me small, to discourage me from exploring the vast, rich, mystical dimensions of faith.

What had once felt like a locked door, bolted by years of indoctrination and fear, now stood wide open — a path stretching ahead, calling me forward.

Religious Indoctrination vs. Spiritual Belief

I began to understand, in a way I never had before, the profound difference between what I had been taught and what I was now living.

Religious indoctrination, as I came to see it, was built on clear doctrines, rigid rules, and unquestionable dogmas - Control. Authority figures — priests, sacred texts, the institution itself — decided what was true and what was forbidden. It emphasized obedience, tradition, and often cloaked itself with the use of guilt and fear.

It was a system that told you exactly how to belong, what to believe, how to behave, and it left little room for questions or personal exploration. I remembered the countless times I had been taught you must attend Sunday mass or risk falling from God's grace; if you don't confess your sins, you cannot receive communion; sacred texts are not to be questioned, only followed.

Even small acts of humanity were framed in terms of moral danger. Skipping a service because of exhaustion was "slipping away" from God. Admitting doubt about scripture was "inviting temptation." Expressing your own spiritual experience that didn't align with church teaching was "pride" or "deception." The rules were more than guidelines — they were lifelines you were told could be cut at any moment if you mis stepped.

This was the framework I had grown up in — a framework that kept me small, wrapped in shame and constraint, convinced I would never be enough for the God I was taught to serve. The God I had been given in childhood was more like a stern ruler keeping score than a loving presence.

Spiritual belief — the space I was slowly, tenderly moving into — was something entirely different. Here, the authority was internal. My own intuition, my lived experiences, my direct connection with the Divine became the compass. There was no checklist to prove worthiness, no gatekeeper between me and sacred connection.

It was flexible and evolving, embracing wisdom from many traditions, not just one. I could read the teachings of Jesus alongside the poetry of Rumi, the wisdom of Indigenous elders, or the quiet insights from my own dreams — and find God in all of them.

Instead of fear, it emphasized love, growth, healing, and inner peace. It encouraged me to question, to explore, to listen for what resonated in my own heart without fearing I was betraying something holy.

It gave me permission to see prayer not as kneeling in a pew, but as walking barefoot in the grass, lighting a candle at my kitchen table, or whispering gratitude to the morning sky.

I began to feel the Divine not as a distant, judging figure, but as a living presence all around me — in the rustle of leaves that sounded like whispers, in the deep stillness of meditation, in the songs that stirred something ancient in my soul, and in the small, perfect synchronicities that reminded me I was never truly alone.

The biggest difference became unmistakable: religious indoctrination was something taught, something imposed from the outside. Spiritual belief was something lived, something discovered, something that rose up from within.

I was no longer living under someone else's definition of truth. I was walking, for the first time, into my own.

And most of all, I came to understand that it is different for everyone. We each hold our own evolving, deeply personal version of the Creator — a version shaped by the unique journeys we have walked, the heartbreaks we have survived, the questions we have dared to ask, and the lessons we are still here to learn.

No two paths are the same, and no two visions of the Divine need to match. Some find God in churches filled with incense and hymns. Some find God in the forest, where the wind becomes the choir and the trees the cathedral pillars. Some find God in the stillness of meditation or the sweat of a long run. Others hear God in the whispered wisdom of ancestors, or in the fierce resilience that has carried them through loss and pain.

That, I realized, is not only okay — it is sacred. It is the beauty of being human: to discover and shape a spirituality that truly fits the contours of your own life.

The version of God I was taught was no longer for me. I know for many, it still works. That's okay. I don't try to convince them otherwise. I allow them the grace to embrace those beliefs that work for them, just as I have embraced what now works for me.

The God I Was Taught vs. The Divine I Now Know

The God I was taught to know was a distant figure, a man in the sky, a long, white-robed Father seated high above, always watching, always judging. He was the gatekeeper, the punisher, the enforcer of rules. He demanded obedience, submission, repentance — especially from women.

My voice was too loud, I was told.

My grief was too messy.

My anger was sinful.

My questions were rebellion.

My body was a temptation.

The God I was taught about offered love, but under certain conditions — only if you followed the rules, confessed your sins, and carried your cross without complaint. Heaven was the reward, however now, here, in this life, you were expected to suffer, to bear the weight of your failures, to prove yourself worthy.

The God I have come know — the Divine Presence I have come to sense — lives in my bones, in my breath, in my grief, in my rising. Encompassing the very essence of who I am, without asking anything of me.

She — or He — or They — are beyond gender, beyond human form, beyond the limitations we try to place on the Sacred. They simply ARE.

The Divine does not wait with judgment for my imperfection. She holds space for my falling and my rising — again and again.

She weeps with me in my sorrow.

It rages with me at the injustice.

He laughs with me in my joy.

She remembers the one I was — before the world taught me to shrink, before religion taught me to fear my own being, before shame wrapped its cold fingers around my spirit. She knew me long before I knew myself. And She has waited, unwavering, for my remembering.

This Divine presence speaks to me in quiet whispers — in synchronicities that remind me I am never alone, in the moonlight that softens the darkest nights, in the sudden rush of intuition that pulses through my chest and says, "Yes, this way, trust this."

She does not ask me to kneel in submission. She asks me to stand in communion. To meet Her in the raw, trembling places of my life and say, "Here I am — whole, messy, human, beloved."

Above all, I realized something life-altering: I did not lose my faith. I awakened it. I gathered it back — pulling together the scattered pieces I had been told were unworthy, unholy, unacceptable. I drew them close, dusted them off, and made them whole again. I stopped listening to what I was told was right or wrong and instead tuned in to what resonated within me.

I no longer measure my worth by the old rules or the old judgments. I no longer seek the Divine in someone else's image. I carry faith within me — as part of me, as the truest, fiercest, most luminous part of who I am.

I'm making myself whole again.

Looking Ahead

This chapter of my life — this spiritual awakening, this shift from doctrine to direct experience — wasn't about discarding God. It was about listening to a Creator in a new, more intimate, more expansive form. It was no longer the God of fear, control, or ritualized obligation — it was a Divine presence that met me in the raw, unguarded places of my life.

For so many years, I felt that everything that went wrong was because I did something wrong. I was being punished. I wasn't holy enough. I wasn't living at the level expected by my God. How the religious indoctrinations made me feel less than.

Yet, over time, something began to shift.

Not a God who demands sacrifice, but a Creator who restores—who gathers the broken pieces of our souls with gentle hands, who breathes life into what we thought was lost, who invites us not to fear or punishment but to healing and wholeness. A presence that mends what's torn, rekindles what's dimmed, and welcomes us back with open arms, reminding us that we are always enough, always loved, always worthy of grace.

Not a God locked behind rituals, pews, and pulpits; a Creator who dances beside me in the moonlight, whispers softly in moments of stillness, and reminds me with every heartbeat: I was never truly alone.

When I say "God" now, I mean the Presence that held me when nothing else could. Not because I obeyed every rule, recited every prayer, or fit neatly into someone else's mold of devotion — but because I dared to fall apart, to question, to rage, to doubt, and still returned to love. This God, this Divine energy, welcomes my whole self — my grief, my laughter, my longing, my becoming.

My questioning.

This, I believe, is the essence of faith — not blind obedience, but brave, open-hearted seeking. It is the willingness to step into the unknown, to trust the stirrings of your own soul, and to follow the path that calls you even when it defies the rules you were taught.

And it is only the beginning.

As I stand under the night sky, I feel the cool air on my skin and the steady beat of my heart — as if the universe was breathing with me, reassuring me I am safe even as everything familiar fell away.

In that quiet moment, I understood: my journey is not about arriving at fixed answers, but about allowing myself to expand, to evolve, to keep reaching for deeper truths.

The sky above, the earth below, the breath within — all remind me I am cradled in something vast and loving. And for now, at this moment, I am blessed.

Blessed to be at peace with the knowledge I hold, knowing that as I continue to grow, learn, and walk this path, my beliefs will grow alongside me.

When God Went Silent

Chapter Eight:
Shadows I'm Still Unraveling —
What was Taken from Me

"The shadows we carry are not our failures;
they are the stories we wrapped around our hearts to survive."

Shadows

As part of reshaping my spiritual landscape, I learned to look inward — not just at what I believed, but at the emotional and psychological patterns that still shaped my daily life.

I realized that even with my evolving spirituality, there were shadows inside me: old wounds, survival mechanisms, and buried emotions that had shaped how I loved, how I trusted, how I showed up in the world.

I was ready to face these shadows — not with shame, but with deep curiosity and compassion.

I was ready to ask: What patterns am I still holding onto out of fear? What parts of myself have I kept locked away because I believed they weren't lovable, spiritual, or worthy?

Above all, what would it mean to unravel these knots, to let these old patterns go, and to meet myself — without pretense — on the other side?

I used to think the shadows in my life were failures. The parts of me I wanted to hide — the anger, the fear, the grief, the patterns I couldn't seem to break — I saw them as flaws, as proof that something inside me was wrong or unfinished.

But as I've walked deeper into my healing, I've come to understand something far more tender, far more profound: My shadows are not my failures.

They are the survival threads that kept me alive when I didn't know how to live. They are the quiet agreements I made with myself in order to endure. They are the old stories, the inherited wounds, the protective layers I wove around my heart so that I could keep moving forward, even when life shattered me.

These shadows — the ones I am still unraveling — are not here to shame me.

They are here to be seen.

To be honored.

To be gently unspooled, like knots I once tied so tightly, believing they were necessary for my safety.

I am not unraveling them because I failed.

I am unraveling them because I have *survived*.

Because I have arrived at a place in my journey where I no longer need to live bound by these old defenses. Because I am ready — finally — to see what's been hidden, to hold it with compassion, and to ask:

What can I release now?

What can I set down?

What version of myself am I ready to meet on the other side of this unraveling?

This chapter goes beyond just grief or anger. It is about reclaiming all the pieces of myself I once tucked away, believing they didn't fit into the life or the faith I was supposed to live.

It is about becoming whole — not solely on emotional and spiritual levels. Because this isn't just about emotional shadows; it's also about the shadows of faith, of meaning, of how I understand the Divine and my place in the universe.

Let's step into the dark together, not to be consumed by it — but to reclaim the pieces of myself that have been waiting in the shadows all along.

The Shadow of Restlessness

Grief and anger left me sleepless, my body coiled tight like a spring wound far past its limit.

It wasn't tension I felt — I was tension itself.

Every muscle held the memory of loss; every breath carried the imprint of fear. My shoulders ached from the invisible weight I carried; my chest felt clenched, as if bracing against a blow that hadn't yet arrived but surely would.

Even after the initial storm of grief subsided — after the funeral, after the paperwork, after the long days of managing survival — I couldn't unwind.

I remained hypervigilant, locked in a state of constant readiness. It was as if my nervous system had been permanently rewired: alert for danger, tuned to every small shift, every hint of threat. Somewhere deep inside, I believed that if I ever softened, if I ever let my guard down, the world would blindside me again.

My mind became a relentless machine, spinning through endless loops. I anticipated every possibility, rehearsed every worst-case scenario, strategized for disasters that hadn't happened yet.

I planned.

I over prepared.

I braced.

I waited.

No amount of planning could quiet the part of me that lived in fear.

When I did manage to close my eyes, the worst of it arrived. I wasn't greeted by sleep — I was ambushed by memory.

Each time my eyelids fluttered shut, I saw him.

Not the man I loved in life, not the partner I had shared laughter and dreams with — but the still body I had found that night, wrapped in blankets, lifeless on the floor. The image replayed again and again, searing itself into my vision, flooding every attempt at rest with horror and disbelief.

Even in the dark, even in the softness of a pillow, there was no safety.

My mind pulled me back to that moment: the shock, the screaming, the desperate attempts to wake him, the primal sound that tore from my own throat.

It was as if my nervous system didn't know how to stand down, didn't know how to unclench, didn't know how to stop bracing for the next wave of devastation. This wasn't merely exhaustion of the body — it was a hollowing of the spirit.

My body was in survival mode, but my soul was starving for rest, for gentleness, for the kind of quiet that allows you to heal. Yet, I couldn't reach it.

Not yet.

Not then.

The cost of this? My rest. My peace. My body's natural rhythms — the slow inhale and exhale of trust, the sweet surrender of deep sleep, the soft unfolding of a body at ease — were stolen by the constant need to stay on alert. I forgot what it felt like to relax fully, to let my shoulders drop, to close my eyes without the tension of dread humming right below the surface.

Grief and anger became more than emotional states — they turned physical. They lived in my skin, in my bones, in my breath. And though they had once served me, once kept me moving forward when collapse seemed inevitable, they also trapped me. They robbed me of presence. They stole the quiet, nourishing moments that allow a body and a soul to heal.

Now, I am learning to reclaim that rest, step by step.

To remind my body it is safe.

To teach my heart it no longer has to stand guard every moment of the day.

This is not easy work. It is work that asks me to lay down old armor, to trust again, to believe that not every quiet night will end in disaster.

I know this: I cannot fully heal without rest. And I deserve to heal.

I deserve to live a life where rest is not earned through exhaustion but granted because I am human, because I am worthy, because I am still here.

The Shadow of Lost Softness

In wielding anger as armor, I locked out tenderness — not only from others, but from myself.

It wasn't intentional.

It wasn't cruel.

It was survival.

Vulnerability became terrifying; not because it hurt, but because it felt like a risk I couldn't take.

I was afraid that if I opened myself to feeling, if I opened too wide, I would shatter — scatter into pieces too small to gather back again. So, I stayed guarded. I kept the doors closed. I didn't let anyone in. I couldn't let them see the struggle. Because if I did… I might never be able to close the hurt back in.

I had to stay strong, because there was a voice inside whispering, *You've barely held it together this long. If you let go — if you fall apart — you may never find your way back.*

So, I stayed strong. I stayed guarded.

I became the woman who could handle it, the one who held it all, the one others leaned on — even as I longed to collapse into someone else's arms, to be the one held for once. I wore strength like armor, but beneath it, I was a quiet wreck — shattered in places no one ever looked

As the only parent left for my children, I held everything together — for them. I had to be the steady one, the strength, the soft place to land, so they could collapse. So they could grieve. So they didn't have to carry what I did.

Here's the shadow I didn't see for a long time: in staying armored, I wasn't just keeping pain out — I was keeping love out, too.

I wasn't shielding myself from heartbreak — I was shielding myself from softness, from intimacy, from the sweet vulnerability that lets us be seen.

I lost the part of myself that once allowed me to receive love freely, to trust without flinching, to surrender without fearing loss.

I lost the ease that once let me rest my head on another's shoulder without calculating the risk.

I lost the softness that made room for joy to flow in, for comfort to wrap around me, for tenderness to touch the raw places inside without setting off alarms.

This is the shadow I am still working to unravel. Because I know now that strength without softness is brittle. Those walls meant to protect can also imprison. That surviving isn't the same as living — and living, real living requires an open heart.

My spiritual work has been slowly, painfully, beautifully teaching me this: That true strength includes softness.

That true resilience includes surrender.

That the bravest thing I can do now is not to stay armored, but to dare to let myself be loved again — fully, wildly, vulnerably, knowing I may break, but trusting that I can also mend.

This is not easy. I am still learning how to take the armor off, piece by piece. I am still learning how to sit in the tenderness without panicking, how to let love touch me without pulling away.

Every time I lean into softness, every time I let myself receive, I reclaim a part of myself I thought was lost forever.

That, I believe, is where real healing begins.

The Shadow of Presence Lost to the Past

Anger and grief have a way of pulling you backward.

Tethering your heart and mind to what was — the moments you can't relive. The words you didn't say. The life that existed before everything you knew changed.

They keep you there, instead of letting you be with what is.

I became trapped in relentless mental spirals — replaying old wounds, revisiting past conversations, turning over betrayals in my mind like stones I couldn't stop picking up. Every quiet moment became an invitation to slip back into memory, to ask the unanswerable: Why did this happen? What did I miss? What else could I have done?

Layered into all of that was the most agonizing absence of all — the not knowing.

My husband's death was not explained, not ever resolved. No further details shared to ease the relentless question. Suicide or homicide?

It mattered. For me, it mattered.

It shaped how I grieved.

It shaped how I understood the loss. It shaped how I tried to move forward. The unanswered questions hovered, whispering possibilities. They might ease the weight of guilt I carried. The fear that I was the catapult. That my version of tough love was too much for him to bear.

The sheriff's office gave no clear answers, no closure, no path forward. I live with the torment of a cold case, haunted not just by loss, but by mystery, by injustice, by the gaping silence where truth should have been.

The cost was steep.

While my mind lived in those past landscapes, my present life continued unfolding without me.

Precious moments slipped through my fingers: the warmth of my son's laughter, the softness of a shared meal, the beauty of an ordinary sunrise. I was there in body but not in mind — burdened by old pain, caught in old stories.

The people I loved were still here, still reaching for me, but I couldn't reach back because part of me was frozen in a world that no longer existed.

Grief and anger narrowed my vision, pulling my attention away from what was alive, vibrant, and possible.

And though those emotions once served a purpose — helping me process, helping me survive — they also became a cage. I realize now that presence is not something to take for granted.

Presence is a gift.

Presence is practice.

Presence is choice I have to make, again and again, to bring my attention back to what is real, right now.

To let go of what I cannot change. To honor the past without living inside it. To meet the people in front of me — and myself — with the fullness of my presence, knowing that this moment is all I have.

The Shadow of False Control

In the aftermath of loss, I clung to control like a lifeline — a trembling hand grasping for something solid in the rubble of everything I had known.

Control gave me the illusion of safety.

I believed that if I stayed angry, if I stayed sharp, if I anticipated every threat and guarded every door, I could protect myself from further devastation. I convinced myself that vigilance was strength, that hyper-awareness was wisdom, that tightening my grip on life would somehow prevent it from slipping away again.

I see now, control became a cage. A prison I built for myself out of fear. It isolated me from the people who longed to come close. It shut out the very love I ached for, because I was too busy preparing for the next blow, too busy scanning the horizon for the next loss. Making sure every T was crossed and every I dotted in every situation, in life itself.

I longed for true connection, for tenderness, for ease — but I had walled myself in so tightly that even when love knocked gently at my door, I strained to hear it. It was there, but for a long time, kept at arm's length.

The hardest part of healing wasn't the grief; it was the surrender. It was loosening my clenched fists. It was allowing myself to admit that no matter how sharp my edges, no matter my preparation, life would still be unpredictable.

People would still leave. Things would still fall apart. Pain would still find me. But so could joy. So could connection. So could surprise, and beauty, and softness — if only I allowed myself to stop gripping so tight and let life flow again.

True healing, I've come to realize, doesn't come from controlling every outcome but from stepping beyond fear and control to allow space for possibility.

It comes from trust — trust in the unfolding, trust in myself, trust in the unseen forces that guide us even when we can't see the full path ahead.

Control made me feel safe. Surrender is what set me free. Free to live life without limits, to be present in each moment.

The Shadows of Love and Trust

Even now, with all the spiritual work I have done, there are shadows I have to consciously titrate through — tender, raw places I've circled for years but haven't yet stepped into.

The most difficult of these is allowing love into my life without fear of loss.

For so long, I have protected myself behind built walls, forged from past heartbreak, grief, and the silent promise that I would never again let someone close enough to shatter me.

Love feels beautiful — yes — but it also feels dangerous. It can build you up and hold you steady, yet it can also shatter you into pieces you no longer recognize.

My heart remembers what it's like to be left. To watch everything I built collapse. To stand in the ashes, wondering how I'll ever trust again. I know what it feels like to watch a casket lowered into the earth with a part of you in it.

As a result, I keep my armor up. I smile. I give. I care — yet only to a point. There's always a part of me bracing, preparing for the moment it all slips away.

Now, I am working to let the walls down. To let people in. To embrace love without fear of it being torn from me again.

To risk closeness, knowing that love always carries the possibility of loss — but that the alternative is a life half-lived, a heart half-open.

Alongside love, I am still unraveling the shadow of trust.

Trust that I will not be left again.

Trust that even if I am left, I will survive.

Knowing I stand strong within myself, without bending or breaking for the sake of keeping someone beside me.

This is the hardest work, the most delicate thread I am pulling now — because it touches the deepest wound: the fear that I am not enough, or that I am too much, or that love will abandon me when I begin to believe in it.

Yet, even here, my spiritual path is guiding me.

It reminds me that love is not earned through perfection.

That trust is not given only when all risk is gone.

That real, soul-deep connection begins when I stop hiding, stop shrinking, stop pretending I don't need.

These are the shadows I still face daily — gently, bravely, one breath at a time.

The Shadow of What God Actually Is

Perhaps the deepest, most tender shadow I am still unraveling is this: What is the true nature of God — and where does God fit in my life now?

For most of my life, I clung to the God I was taught: the all-knowing Father in the sky, the keeper of commandments, the dispenser of punishment and reward. This God watched, judged, and waited. He was the God of my childhood, the God of my mother's prayers, the God who hovered over every decision with a silent ledger.

Yet, when life cracked me open — when grief hollowed me out, when the people I loved were taken, when the prayers I whispered were met with silence — I began to feel the edges of that image crumble.

The God I was taught no longer fit inside the aching, raw, trembling space of my actual life. Because how could He?

How could a distant, rule-keeping deity carry me through the dark nights when I lay shattered on the floor, begging for comfort?

How could the God of punishment offer tenderness when all I needed was to be wrapped in mercy?

How could the God of obedience make sense of the wild, messy, beautiful unfolding of who I was — not as a perfect believer, but as a human being, scarred and sacred all at once?

This is the shadow I still sit with today. It's the shadow of letting go — of peeling away the layers of religious indoctrination, of loosening my grip on the God I was taught to cling to, of daring to wonder if the Divine I now know might be something softer, fuller, freer.

Because the Creator I now feel is not a man on a throne. She is the breath in my lungs. He is the pulse in my veins. They are the quiet presence that meets me in dreams, in synchronicities, in the hush between heartbeats.

This Creator is not waiting for me to earn love — this Creator **is** love. This Creator is not testing my worthiness — this Creator has always, always called me worthy.

Yet…part of me still trembles. Still wonders: Am I allowed to believe this? Am I betraying my roots? Am I stepping too far into the unknown? Who will I be if I let go of the scaffolding of old beliefs, the ones that shaped my childhood, my family, my earliest understanding of life and death and meaning?

Here's the truth I'm learning—step by step, with patience and grace: There is no guidebook for this. No priest, no pastor, no elder can hand me the perfect map.

This path has to be lived. It has to be felt. It has to be learned, step by trembling step, by my own soul, in my own time, in my own way.

This is not easy work.

It is not finished work.

It is sacred work.

I am learning to trust the Creator who lives in the quiet spaces, the Creator who holds me when I crumble, the Creator who doesn't demand perfection but invites presence, the A

Creator who exists not only beyond, but within — woven into every breath I take, every longing I feel, every rising I live.

Closing Reflection

These shadows are not punishments, nor are they failures.

They are the old guards, the old protectors, the patterns that helped me survive — a cross emotional and spiritual dimensions

They were shaped not only by life's hardships, but by the religious frameworks I once clung to, the doctrines that taught me to be small, to be obedient, to carry guilt and silence as proof of goodness.

My shadows were not only born of personal wounds, but of spiritual ones — inherited teachings that told me who I could and could not be.

Yes, they took from me.

They stole my rest, my softness, my presence, my trust.

They tangled me in grief loops, locked me in cycles of control, and at times, left me feeling separated from the very God I longed to touch.

They also gave me something: resilience, determination, righteous anger, and the fierce love that kept me standing when everything fell apart. They were not signs of failure — they were signs of survival.

Survival is no longer enough — I am here for more.

I am here to live.

To soften.

To love.

To be loved.

To trust.

To allow.

To step fully into the woman I was always meant to be —
not as defined by a church, a doctrine, or a rigid set of rules,
but as defined by the Divine presence I now know personally,
intimately, expansively.

Spiritually, I am reclaiming my wholeness.

I am stepping out of the old beliefs that said faith requires
perfection, submission, or self-erasure.

I am stepping into a spiritual relationship that is alive,
evolving, and deeply woven into my own soul's truth. I no
longer bow out of fear; I rise in reverence. I no longer follow
teachings that shrink me; I follow the Divine call that expands
me.

These shadows — the ones I name now — are no longer
here to rule me. I can honor them for what they once offered,
and gently lay them down, one by one, without shame.

I am free to create a life, a love, and a spirituality that reflect
the fullness of who I am becoming.

Here, right here, is where my real faith begins.

Not in the doctrines I inherited, but in the living, breathing
connection I am daring to build — with myself, with the
Divine, with the great mystery that has always, always been
holding me.

This is not the end of the work.

This is the sacred middle — the place where healing and
becoming meet. I am worthy of every trembling, radiant step.

Chapter Nine:
What Righteous Anger Gave Me

"My anger didn't burn me down —
it made me blaze hard enough
to break the chains off my own damn wrists."

When Grief Caught Fire

Righteous anger is not the same as bitterness or mere frustration — it is a holy, fire-lit force that rises when something sacred has been violated.

Nothing prepares you for the kind of violation that comes with sudden death.

When someone you love is taken without warning, righteous anger is no longer an idea — it becomes embodied.

It lives in your bones. It howls in the silence. It surges in the gap between what should have been and what will never be.

It is the fierce, protective energy that says, *No more.*

The pulse that rises in the face of betrayal, injustice, and deep loss — not to destroy, but to defend; not to lash out blindly, but to stand for what is right, for what matters, for what must not be lost.

For me, righteous anger was not a feeling — it was a survival force. It began shaping how I moved through the world, how I interacted with life itself. Especially when there were no answers. No explanation for why a life was extinguished in the first place.

When grief hollowed me out, when heartbreak threatened to pull me under, when the weight of everything I had lost pressed me to the ground, it was anger that surged through my bones and kept me upright.

It whispered, *Get up. Keep going. Fight for yourself, for your children, for the truth, for the life you still have.* This anger did not shrink me — it forged me.

This chapter is not a repeat of the shadows I named before. This is the other side: the place where I explore what anger gave me, how it strengthened me, how it reshaped not only my emotional landscape but also my spiritual path.

121

It's not about rage or heartbreak — it's about the deeper transformation that happens when you let anger be a tool for growth rather than destruction. It's about how grief, when paired with righteous fire, can become a catalyst for reclaiming your voice, your power, and your sacred worth.

Let's step into this space together — not to recount the pain, but to honor the fire that shaped who I am becoming.

It Gave Me Survival Fuel

When grief threatened to paralyze me, when the weight of unanswered questions suffocated me, when exhaustion clawed at my every step — it was anger that kept me moving.

Anger became my fuel, a raw, relentless energy coursing through me when everything else had run dry. It was not gentle or graceful; it was fierce, demanding, sometimes even harsh.

It kept me upright when I wanted to crumble. It whispered in my ear: You cannot quit.

You cannot let this be the end of your story.

You will not be defined by this loss alone.

Anger carried me through the moments that should have broken me: the endless funeral arrangements, the painful phone calls to family, the unbearable legal paperwork and formalities that felt impossible to face.

It pushed me through every bit of life when I was too drained to fight. It gave me a backbone when I had to confront the financial collapse, the heartbreak of losing not just a partner but a home, a shared future, a sense of stability.

It braced me through the sleepless nights when loneliness pressed in, when fear crept at the edges of my mind, when the house felt far too quiet and the bed far too big.

Most of all, it became my companion on the long, lonely nights of single parenting, when I had to show up —

exhausted, grieving, hollowed out — and still be present for my child.

Without that fire, I don't know how I would have survived. It was anger, not serenity, that reminded me I still mattered, that my voice still counted, that I had a right to stand up and keep going even when the world felt like it had abandoned me.

That anger was not my enemy — it was the part of me that refused to let life swallow me whole.

It was the fierce, protective force that said: You are still here. And as long as you are here, you will not give up.

This righteous anger was not about vengeance or bitterness; it was about survival. It was about reclaiming my place in a world that felt shattered, about pushing back against the tide that threatened to drown me, about lighting a fire when everything else had gone dark.

It was the spark in my chest that said: You have endured too much to stop now.

You will rise.

You will keep rising.

It Gave Me a Stronger Voice

Before loss reshaped me, I had learned — like so many women — to soften my truth. To shrink my opinions so they wouldn't ruffle feathers. To smooth my edges so no one would feel threatened.

I apologized when I wasn't wrong — for things that didn't matter, for things that weren't mine to carry, for the simplest and most ridiculous reasons.

I accepted less than I deserved because I didn't want to be "difficult." I told myself it was better to keep the peace, better to be agreeable, better to hold my tongue.

Then came the fire — anger, righteous and fierce. Anger at the countless injustices that crossed my path, at all the ways I was told to stay small, quiet, and compliant.

Anger shattered that silence.

It didn't ask for permission, and it didn't wait for the right moment — it surged up, fierce and uncompromising, demanding to be heard.

I found myself saying things I would have once swallowed. I stopped minimizing my needs, no longer content sitting quietly in the corner. I stopped excusing harm, no longer willing to smooth over the ways I had been overlooked, dismissed, or hurt. I stopped accepting crumbs from people or institutions that wanted me grateful for scraps.

I stopped being the baby of the family who merely followed directions. I began to express my thoughts. Not with finesse. Not with style. With the fierce, righteous anger I had been holding back for decades. It came out messy. Loud. Unapologetic. Ugly, even. And still — necessary.

This voice is one of the reasons I no longer speak to my siblings. I spoke my truth for the first time and instead of being heard, I was dismissed. My voice wasn't honored — it was ignored. When they couldn't control my tone, they tried to control my choices.

That was when I realized: my silence had served them. My voice disrupted the dynamic they preferred.

Anger taught me something that years of quiet endurance never could:

Silence is not peace.

Silence is suppressive.

It is a slow erasure of the self.

I had been trained to avoid conflict at all costs. To prioritize harmony over honesty. To equate speaking up with being unsafe.

So, when my voice finally emerged, it didn't come with finesse. It came from a nervous system no longer willing to tolerate being ignored.

My body, once tight with swallowed words, began to loosen. My chest, once compressed with unspoken needs, began to breathe again.

Liberation, too, has its shadows.

Speaking truth, especially after years of silence, can hit hard. It can shock those who were used to my compliance. It can fracture relationships that were never built to hold my fullness.

On an emotional level, it was devastating to realize that some people only loved the version of me who kept quiet. Some only stayed close because I never challenged them.

Finding my voice wasn't about raising the volume — it was about raising the stakes. It was about learning to stand in my truth even when it was uncomfortable, even when it risked conflict, even when it meant letting people walk away.

It was about knowing that my worth did not come from being agreeable, but from being authentic.

This strong voice didn't just serve me in arguments or confrontations — it served me in the quiet moments too, when I needed to choose myself.

It served me in boundaries I never thought I'd be strong enough to hold.

It served me when I advocated for myself in spaces where I once would have stayed silent.

It served me when I chose to tell my story, with openness and truth, even when that story was messy, complicated, and full of emotions that made people uneasy.

My voice is not about proving I'm better. It's not about forcing my thoughts on anyone or demanding that my opinions be followed. It isn't rooted in ego or superiority — it's rooted in a deep, burning need to be heard. To be seen. To be acknowledged as worthy of space, even if you don't agree with me.

I'm not asking for validation — I'm demanding the basic respect of being listened to, instead of being made to feel small, silenced, dismissed, or simply having a voice at all.

Anger became the spark that lit up my throat.

Grief became the force that cleared the debris.

Somewhere between them, I found a voice that had been waiting my whole life to speak.

Speak.

Be seen.

Take up space.

Not because it's easy, but because you were never meant to disappear.

It Gave Me the Courage to Reclaim Myself

For years — maybe for most of my life — I followed the rules.

Not because I believed them, because my safety and worth seemed to depend on them. I knew what was expected of me: be the good wife, the good mother, the good Catholic woman. I was taught that obedience was love, that sacrifice was holiness, and that staying small was virtue.

So, I adapted.

I wore those roles like a garment sewn with care, one thread woven after another by family, church, culture, and tradition.

The thread of silence.

The thread of self-denial.

The thread of "don't ask, simply accept."

I tried to make myself palatable. Pleasant. Predictable. I adjusted myself to fit the rooms I entered. I said yes when I meant no. I swallowed questions I wasn't allowed to ask.

Then came the breaking.

Grief didn't just rip someone I loved out of my life — it tore through the image I had spent decades maintaining. Loss didn't knock politely. It gutted me.

And in the hollowed-out aftermath, all the roles I had tried so hard to perform suddenly felt unbearable. The identity I had clung to — the one that had been rewarded by others, praised as faithful and selfless — now felt like a prison made of my own skin.

It was disorienting. There's a strange kind of terror that comes when you realize the life you've built was shaped around survival, not truth. When the blueprint you were given no longer fits, but you don't yet know how to build something new. I felt unmoored. Uncertain. Like I was floating between who I had been and who I wasn't yet brave enough to become.

And then... anger.

Not the petty kind.

Not the outburst kind.

The sacred kind.

The kind that arrives when you've been quiet too long. The kind that comes from centuries of silenced women humming in your blood. The kind that doesn't destroy — it awakens.

It compelled me to fight — and, more importantly, allowed me to question.

It was anger that gave me the courage to look at the systems I had once accepted without hesitation — religious, cultural, relational — and ask:

Do I still believe this?

Do I still want this?

Does this serve the woman I am becoming, or does it keep her buried?

Anger lit up the places I had been too afraid to question. The rules I had followed without consent. The identities I had performed without authenticity.

It whispered truths I hadn't dared to believe before:

You don't have to play small to be good.

You don't have to bow down to be worthy.

You don't have to follow a path that no longer leads you home.

This reclamation was both liberating and brutal. I grieved the comfort of certainty even as I outgrew it.

I mourned the version of myself who did everything right, only to still end up broken. I felt rage and relief intertwine — one burning away the old, the other making room for the new.

My anger reached beyond religion, beyond family, beyond culture. I was angry that I had spent so long suppressing the very voice that now felt like the truest part of me.

In that fire, something else emerged:

I began to reclaim myself.

Not with bitterness — but with clarity. Not with rebellion — but with truth.

I peeled off the labels one by one. I let the old definitions fall away: obedient, good, nice, unquestioning. I began to realize that my spirituality wasn't something handed to me by an institution — it was something alive inside me, something I could tend and nurture on my own terms.

I no longer wanted to be someone else's idea of a good woman. I wanted to be whole.

I began to realize I had the power to choose: my beliefs, my values, my rhythm, and the way I walk with the Divine — on my own terms, in my own time.

On a spiritual level, this wasn't abandonment — it was a return.

To my body.

To my soul.

To a kind of knowing I had been taught to distrust.

Anger wasn't the opposite of faith — it was the beginning of authentic faith. It cracked open the shell of who I thought I had to be and gave me permission to explore who I actually was underneath. It led me to a more intuitive, more personal, more soul-led spirituality — one not shaped by obedience, but by resonance.

Now...

I no longer pray because I was told to. I pray because my soul needs to speak.

I no longer follow rituals because they're expected. I follow the ones that bring my body peace and make my spirit feel alive.

I no longer measure myself against rules that were never made for my liberation. I measure myself by presence, truth, and alignment.

This voice — the one I reclaimed through the fire — still trembles sometimes.

It's not always eloquent. It's not always filtered. It is mine. That, more than anything else, is what healing has become for me:

Not fixing. Not erasing. Reclaiming.

Reclaiming the right to belong to myself — fully, fiercely, and without apology.

Anger gave me the courage to step outside the lines and carve a new path. And on that path, I am learning to walk in my own name, in my own power, in my own sacred light.

It Gave Me a Deep Sense of Justice

Before loss reshaped me, my sense of fairness was often quiet, polite, and easily set aside. I wanted to be understanding, forgiving, flexible — the peacemaker, the one who absorbed tension rather than created it.

But when everything broke, when grief cracked my chest open and anger surged through the rawness left behind, I began to feel something fierce rise within me: a sharpened sense of justice.

Anger clarified for me what I was willing to stand for — and what I would never, ever tolerate again. It made my boundaries unmistakable.

It showed me what was nonnegotiable: the dignity of my own heart, the safety of my children, the sovereignty of my spiritual path.

I became the fierce protector of what mattered.

Anger became the voice inside that said:

No, you will not disrespect me.

No, you will not cross this line.

No, you will not dismiss my pain or silence my truth.

It wasn't about being reactive; it was about discovering a sacred determination to defend what was most precious.

Anger helped me name what was worth guarding: my worth, my children's well-being, the tender new shape of my healing, the spiritual journey I was daring to walk.

It taught me that boundaries are not walls of punishment; they are fences of protection, of love, of care. They tell the world: This is what I honor. This is what I will no longer allow to be harmed.

Anger became my sacred ally in this. It helped me stand taller, clearer, more rooted. It helped me draw lines I had once been too afraid to draw. It helped me say yes to what nourished me and a firm, unwavering no to what depleted or disrespected me.

In this way, anger was not a personal fire — it became a force of sacred justice. It aligned me with a fierceness that was not about revenge, but about integrity.

It reminded me that loving myself, protecting my family, and guarding my path were not selfish acts — they were holy acts.

I now see that my anger didn't make me hard or bitter; it made me fierce and clear.

It carved out a new space where love could flourish, not as a passive sentiment, but as an active, protective force.

It taught me that true justice starts inside: when we honor ourselves, when we refuse to betray our own hearts, when we rise in fierce love for who we are and who we are becoming.

Honoring the Sacred Fire

This chapter is not about glorifying anger or pretending that it didn't take a toll on me.

I know the cost intimately.

I know the restless nights, the sleepless hours, the tension that settled into my shoulders like a permanent weight. I know the way my jaw clenched, the way my chest tightened, the way my body became a container for fight energy that had nowhere to go. I know the way anger narrowed my vision at times, making me see only the injustice, only the pain, only the threat.

Today — standing on the other side of the storm, with clearer eyes and a softer heart — I choose to honor what anger gave me.

It gave me survival.

It gave me a raw, unyielding force when everything else inside me wanted to collapse.

It gave me the grit to rise, the fire to keep walking, the courage to speak up when silence would have crushed me.

It gave me strength. Not polished, picture-perfect strength, but the kind of strength forged in chaos — the strength of a woman who has walked through fire and come out scarred but unbroken.

It showed me what I could endure, what I could carry, what I could survive.

It gave me clarity.

It burned away the lies I had once told myself — that I had to be small to be loved, that I had to be quiet to belong, that I had to accept harm to prove my worthiness. It clarified what mattered and what no longer had a place in my life.

It gave me a voice. Anger cracked open the silence that had bound me for years. It pushed me to speak, to claim, to name what was true — even when my voice shook, even when the words were messy and imperfect.

Now, as I continue walking forward, I am learning how to hold that fire in balance.

Not to snuff it out. Not to let it consume me. But to tend it like a sacred flame — one that warms, that illuminates, that guides, but no longer scorches.

This is the sacred balance of healing: honoring what once protected you, even as you choose to lead with love. I don't have to pretend my anger was a mistake. I don't have to be ashamed that it lived inside me, that it shaped me, that it sometimes roared louder than I knew how to handle.

My righteous anger will always be part of me. It's part of my story. Part of my resilience. Part of the reason I am still here.

It no longer has to be the *only* part. It no longer has to be the loudest voice in the room.

Now, I know I can be fierce without being consumed. I can be strong without being hardened. I can stand in my truth without burning myself to ash.

I honor the fire — and I choose, each day, to walk toward peace, toward softness, toward a life where love leads the way.

Because the real miracle, the real triumph, is not that anger saved me. It's that I am learning, slowly and bravely, to let love save me now.

Letting Love Lead

As I close this chapter, I carry with me the truth that anger was never meant to be my forever home. It was the fire that saved me when the walls collapsed, the force that kept me standing when the ground fell away. It was a teacher, a protector, a fierce companion — but it was never meant to be the place I rest.

Now, I am learning to step into something softer.

Not because I am weaker.

Not because I have surrendered or given up.

But because I know the deeper truth:

It takes far more courage to let love lead.

It takes far more strength to soften, to open, to trust again.

It takes the most daring kind of faith to believe that after loss, after betrayal, after devastation, there is still beauty waiting — and that I am still worthy of receiving it.

The fire of righteous anger will always burn inside me, a sacred ember I carry forward. But now, I choose to tend it with care, to let it guide without consuming, to let it warm without wounding.

This is my promise to myself:

I will honor what anger gave me — and I will walk, one step at a time, toward the life love is still calling me to live.

Chapter Ten:
Breaking the Cross

"I didn't walk away from God.
I walked away from the cage they tried to keep Her in."

Truth Whispers

I didn't leave the church in a blaze of fury.

I didn't renounce God or storm away from the altar.

My exit was much quieter than that — more like a slow exhale. A breath saying the God I was taught was no longer needed to survive.

A steady loosening of something that had once felt like structure, but had grown too tight to breathe in. There wasn't a single moment when I declared I no longer belonged. It was gradual. Like a leaf finally letting go after clinging all season.

This isn't a chapter about bitterness. It's not about burning bridges or scorning tradition. It's about truth — and the kind of truth I've learned is rarely loud.

It doesn't always arrive with thunder or finality. More often, it comes as a whisper — a question you can't stop asking. A sense of friction that won't go away. A quiet ache in your chest during a sermon that once brought you comfort. The feeling that something is no longer aligning, even if you can't yet name why. Truth doesn't always shout. Sometimes, it hums. It comes in whispers, quiet but relentless, asking not to be forced, but to be followed

Truth doesn't arrive in destruction alone. It arrives in whispers from the body, in flashes of knowing, in the way the breeze feels like an answer you didn't know you asked. Sometimes truth is soft. Sometimes it's sacred rage. Most often, it's both. When we listen — not with our ears, but with our whole selves — we meet a Divine.

Not in the walls we were told to worship, but in the space that opens when we dare to leave them behind.

A Faith That Couldn't Hold My Questions

I was a "cradle Catholic" — born and raised in the church.
Baptism. First Communion. Confirmation. Marriage.
Twelve years of Catholic school, stiff uniforms, morning
prayers, the sound of creaky pews and incense hanging in the
air like invisible rules. We learned to kneel with discipline, to sit
with our backs straight, to bow our heads right.

My mother believed fiercely in the value of a Catholic
education. She worked herself to the bone to ensure that each
of her five children attended Catholic school for all twelve
years. It was no small feat. Money was tight, but she made it
happen. That sacrifice — that loyalty — was something I held
in deep respect. It was an act of devotion that didn't come from
faith — it came from love. A love for her God.

Because of that, part of me still carries guilt. I know my
mother would have wanted me to remain in the church — to
honor her effort by honoring the faith she gave so much of
herself to uphold. Even as she lay dying in the ICU, her hands
were clenched in prayer.

From a young age, I carried internal doubts about what I
was taught and witnessed.

I didn't have the words for it then. It wasn't defiance. It
wasn't even doubt. It was more like a soft hum — a quiet,
persistent awareness that not everything I was taught resonated
deep in my bones.

I remember one particular sermon when I was younger.
The priest standing at his pulpit warning us never to try and
contact the dead — never to speak to them, never to visit a
medium, never to "open that door." He said it was dangerous,
sinful, forbidden. We're taught to believe that people like that
— the ones who still feel the presence of their loved ones, who

sense things we can't explain — are speaking to the devil. I didn't feel fear when he spoke. I felt confusion.

Why wouldn't God want me to speak to someone I loved who had passed?

Why can a priest speak to spirit but not us?

What could Spirit possibly be doing on the other side that would deny them the chance to stay connected to the ones they loved? To help ease our grief, if for no other reason than love itself?

I never voiced these thoughts. I learned fast that some questions were better left unasked. I carried them with me like stones in my pocket. Heavy. Quiet. Always there.

That was one of the first cracks.

I remember sitting in the confessional, just tall enough for the seat, listing out my "sins" with flushed cheeks and a racing heart. I hadn't hurt anyone. I hadn't lied or stolen. But I was still expected to find something wrong with myself. Something I had done — or failed to do — that needed forgiving.

I couldn't understand why I had to say it to a man behind a screen. If God was all-knowing, and all-loving, wouldn't a sincere prayer whispered from my pillow be enough? If we speak to God directly and ask for forgiveness it would be granted. At least that is what the nuns were teaching us.

Why did forgiveness require a ritual? Why did grace come with rules?

I began to wonder about the things we weren't taught. The gospels and teachings were excluded. The stories erased from the Bible. The absence of the feminine voice in scripture. The silence of Mary, the absence of the Magdalene, the denial of anything that didn't fit the structure.

Why were women not allowed to be priests? Why were questions themselves treated like rebellion?

No one gave me answers. They gave me doctrine. They gave me repetition.

In my home, the atmosphere didn't allow for much questioning either. My father drank heavily. My parents fought often—loud, bitter arguments that echoed down the hallway and into my bones. I would lie awake at night with my hands clasped under the covers, praying harder than I knew how to explain. I would beg God to make it stop. Beg for peace. For quiet. For a sliver of love in our home.

Please, just make them stop fighting. Please, just fix this.

The yelling continued. The pain stayed.

And the silence from heaven was deafening.

It was then I learned something I couldn't yet articulate: Sometimes, God doesn't answer. Or maybe… maybe the God I was introduced to didn't know how to speak to the ache I was holding.

Still, I stayed faithful. I stayed obedient. I went through the motions. I carried the guilt, the obligation, the identity. I did everything I was supposed to do. That quiet ache didn't go away. Deep down, I started to feel the fracture — not of faith itself, but of the way it had been presented to me.

I didn't know, back then, that the body itself can hear truth. That intuition is a holy language.

No one taught me that. The schools taught structure. The church taught obedience. I would come to learn later that the ache in your chest, the fire in your gut, the lump in your throat — these are sacred messengers.

These are the whispers of the soul.

I would come to learn that when the body tightens during a sermon, when tears rise unprovoked, when a ritual no longer feels safe but instead feels like suffocation — something deeper is speaking.

Spirit doesn't always come in visions. Sometimes, it comes in discomfort. Sometimes, it comes in the quiet rebellion of a child who knows something isn't quite right.

That was me. I didn't have the tools. I didn't have the language. I had the knowing.

In time, that knowing grew too loud to ignore.

Staying for the Children, Drifting for Myself

When I became a mother, I carried the teachings with me — not out of habit, but out of hope. Hope that the foundation I was given, despite its cracks, might still offer my children something solid.

Something that could guide them through a world that is often too harsh and too fast. I enrolled them in religious education at church. I took them to Mass. I celebrated their sacraments with reverence. I taught them prayers. I passed down the rituals I had once performed, believing it might give them what it once gave me: a sense of purpose.

A moral compass.

A belonging.

Even then, something inside me was already drifting.

I would sit in the pews and feel like a guest in my own faith. The homilies that once comforted me now felt distant. The repetition felt hollow. The rituals, though familiar, no longer resonated the same way.

It wasn't loud or dramatic. It was subtle. A shift so slow I barely noticed it — until I couldn't unfeel it anymore.

The only reason I remained in the church as long as I did was because of my children.

I wanted them to have a strong spiritual foundation. I wanted them to understand compassion, responsibility, and reverence for life. I believed Catholicism could still offer them those values, even if I no longer aligned with its dogma. I thought, *If I just hold on long enough to get them all through confirmation, then I've done my part.*

So, I stayed. I sat through sermons that no longer stirred me. I folded my hands out of duty, not desire. I spoke prayers I no longer believed word for word but still believed in spirit. I didn't realize that staying was its own form of sacrifice.

It wasn't until my youngest was to start confirmation class that the realization hit me with quiet clarity: *I had been staying for them, not for me.*

I didn't need to pretend anymore.

I didn't need to sit in pews that made me feel small. I didn't need to hold my breath through rituals that no longer stirred my soul.

I had done what I came to do. I had given my children a foundation. Now, I could choose for myself.

In the stillness that followed, something deeper stirred. Not rebellion. Not rejection. Remembrance.

Remembrance of the voice I had always heard beneath the doctrine but didn't understand.

Remembrance of the self I had silenced to fit into a tradition that no longer fit me.

Remembrance of a Presence who had never needed the walls of a church to reach me.

What I was stepping into was something I later learned to call spiritual sovereignty — the quiet, radical right to define my own connection to the sacred. To speak directly to Spirit without intermediaries. To trust my own questions, my own knowing. To explore truth not because I had turned away from God, but because I was finally turning toward myself.

Leaving the church was never about abandonment.

It was about breathing again.

It was about believing that the Divine was far too expansive to be confined by fear, tradition, or someone else's rules.

From Tradition to Truth: A Gradual Unfolding

My spiritual expansion didn't come with fanfare. There was no lightning bolt moment, no grand epiphany. Curiosity. Gentle nudges. A sense of there must be more.

My current husband, Dave, was already on a spiritual path when we met. Our connection became a shared journey.

In the early days, I brought him to church with us. It was the world I knew, and I wanted to share it. He supported that religion not realizing I only practiced it on the outside. I explained the structure, the rituals, and the prayers. He came with curiosity and respect enthralled with all the symbolism.

As our relationship deepened, so did our conversations.

We started attending psychic fairs. Not because I had a clear agenda — because I was curious. Open. Hungry in a way that surprised me.

We wandered through metaphysical bookstores, running our fingers along the spines of books about energy healing, reincarnation, chakras, and universal law. The smell of incense and old paper lingered in the air like memory. Like home. Crystals shimmered on tables beside tarot cards and angel statues. There were no pews, no priests.

There was something sacred there. And it didn't scare me.

At first, I called it exploring. Deep down, I was remembering. Not learning something brand new but uncovering what had always lived inside me — truths buried beneath doctrine, intuition muffled under years of conditioning.

This wasn't about abandoning God. It was about rediscovering a Divine within me. Not a distant figure in the sky who needed obedience — but a living presence in my breath, my body, my knowing. Not a God who demanded sacrifice, but one who whispered *belonging*.

Journey circles. Spiritual development classes. Energy work. Mediumship. Things I had once been warned against. Things the Church called dangerous.

They didn't feel dangerous. They felt like *freedom*. They felt like *truth*.

We talked about angels, spirit guides, past lives, and soul contracts. We sat in circles with others seeking the same thing; something real, something expansive. Not bound by fear. Not rooted in hierarchy. But grounded in love, curiosity, and direct connection to the sacred.

I remember one moment that still stays with me. We were in a spiritual development group when the speaker asserted — without hesitation — that anyone who took their own life was condemned. That they would not enter heaven. Something in me bristled. The old silence inside me cracked open.

Calm, but unwavering. I said, "No, that's not correct. They are allowed in."

We debated. Not to argue — but to expand. Over time, his stance softened. He researched more and reconsidered. That moment changed something in me. Not because I spoke — but because I was *heard*. Because I witnessed someone's heart open because I trusted my own voice.

That moment was a mirror: I no longer needed to defend my growth. I no longer needed permission to believe differently.

I had become my own spiritual authority.

With that came a deeper knowing: That soul journeys do not follow a single path. Maybe we don't come here to get it right — but to *remember*. To fall and rise. To question and reimagine. To circle back to ourselves again and again until it finally feels like home.

Every grief. Every doubt. Every mistake.

Not detours, but initiations.

Not shameful, but sacred.

This unfolding wasn't about finding all the answers. It was about finally asking the *right* questions — the ones that led me back to myself.

The Cross Didn't Shatter — I Set It Down

The symbolism of the broken crucifix on the cover means everything to me.

It represents the breaking of control. The breaking of silence. The breaking of obedience for the sake of fitting in. The disapproval of rules that exclude when we are preached to accept all people.

It's not an act of defiance for the sake of defiance. It's not a rebellion. It's a reclaiming.

I no longer felt held by the faith that raised me. I felt confined by it. There were too many rules. Too much fear. Too many conditions placed on love, acceptance, and worthiness.

Understand, I do not hate the church. I do not reject it. In fact, I'm thankful for what it gave me: a foundation, a moral compass, a system that got me through some incredibly difficult times. And at those times, it was what I needed. I understand and accept that. We do our best with the tools we have where we are at that time. No more. No less.

Like all foundations, it wasn't meant to be the entire structure. Eventually, I had to build something of my own.

Still — I wouldn't be honest if I didn't say this out loud: I carry anger. Righteous Anger!

Not at the priest who turned me away and denied my husband last rites. Not even at the priest I lied to, just so my husband could be buried in the family plot. No.

My anger is not for individuals.

It is for the institution itself.

For the rigid scaffolding of rules masquerading as love. For the pious declarations of unconditional acceptance that disappear when someone is grieving and outside the lines.

It is those people who are wondering and lost. Those who are so lost that they feel their only solution is to leave this world. Their minds do not function because of the feeling of aloneness. Those are the lost sheep. The ones we should reach out to and embrace no matter what. The ones who needed the last rites, so they knew they were still loved and accepted.

Not rejected.

That is what I was taught for twelve years in school.

The betrayal wasn't loud. It was quiet. A turned back. A withheld sacrament. A silence in the moment I needed mercy most.

I was not asking for doctrine. I was asking for compassion.

What I learned is this: Religious systems may claim to speak for God, but they are not God. They cannot carry the fullness of Spirit because Spirit cannot be contained.

My anger isn't proof of my rebellion. It's proof of my belief that love should *never* be so revoked. It lives in me not because I am bitter, but because I still believe we deserve better.

That anger is not what drives me. But it reminds me.

It reminds me why I left. It reminds me of what I will never return to. It reminds me that the Creator I have found does not discriminate or set boundaries.

What Still Guides Me

I no longer pray in the way I was taught.

There is no kneeling beside my bed, no whispered confessions into the dark, no recitation of memorized verses to a distant sky-bound deity. I no longer feel the need to prove my worth through repetition or to beg for love that was never supposed to be conditional.

Now, I sit in stillness.

I breathe.

I speak straight to Spirit — sometimes aloud, sometimes in the silence of my soul.

This Spirit isn't confined to a single name. Sometimes it feels like Mother/Father God. Sometimes it feels like an ancestor. Sometimes it's the gentle presence of an angel, the protective energy of an ascended master, or the familiar essence of someone I once loved. Sometimes, I don't give it a name at all. It just is. That's enough.

I believe we are always supported — surrounded by a great unseen team of helpers, whisperers, and guardians. But they won't interfere unless invited. Consent is sacred. Free will is honored.

So, I ask. I ask for the help, guidance, peace of mind, calm.

Then, I listen.

Not with my ears, but with my body. With my intuition. With the quiet space beneath my thoughts.

Sometimes the answer is a warmth that rises in my chest. Sometimes it's a song that plays the right moment. Sometimes it's a memory, or a vision, or a feeling that washes through me like a wave from another world.

This is what prayer has become for me: not a performance, but a relationship. Not discipline, but a devotion. Not

something I do to be seen, but something I do to see clearer —
myself, my path, and the Divine presence that moves through
all things.

Sometimes this connection happens with meditation. Other
times in dreams. Sometimes while my hands are deep in soil, or
when I'm stirring soup, or when I'm walking alone in nature
and the wind sings secrets only I can hear.

I've come to believe that creativity is a form of prayer —
that when I make something honest, whether it's a crafting, a
story, or a garden bed, I am in communion with the sacred.
Creation, after all, is the language of the Divine. We are not
separate from it. We are extensions of it.

And from that space of connection has grown something I
didn't always have — compassion.

I no longer judge — not people, not religions, not the paths
they walk to reach their own sense of peace. I don't care what
name someone calls the Divine, or who they love, or how they
practice their faith. That's not my business. That's not my soul's
assignment.

I've learned that I can love people I disagree with. I can
offer respect without agreement. I can set boundaries without
cruelty.

If someone's energy disrupts my peace, I don't engage in
battle. I disengage with grace. I don't need to explain. I don't
need to defend. I choose peace — and that is a sacred act of
devotion, too.

The church once taught me judgment — who was right,
who was wrong, who belonged, who was saved.

Spirituality taught me discernment — the quiet inner
compass that says "yes" or "no" without shame or superiority.

Grace is what remains when righteousness dissolves. Grace
is what rises when we choose understanding over ego. Grace is

what meets us when we finally stop performing and fully allow ourselves to be. When we allow our authentic self to step forward and lead.

This is what guides me now.

Not dogma, but presence.

Not fear, but trust.

Not obedience, but deep, intuitive connection.

If I could go back and speak to the little girl I once was — the one who sat in church with questions she wasn't allowed to ask — I'd take her hand and whisper:

"Keep asking. The questions are holy, too."

To the One Standing In-Between

If you are caught between what you were taught and what you're beginning to feel…

If your prayers no longer sound the same, but your heart still longs for connection…

If you're afraid to disappoint the ones who raised you — the mother who lit candles at the altar, the grandmother who tucked rosary beads beneath her pillow…

If you wonder whether the God of your childhood will recognize the seeker you've become…

Let me say this with clarity, love, and without limits: It's okay to outgrow your container. You were never meant to remain the same. You were born to expand. To question. To evolve.

Let the guilt rise if it must. Let the fear speak its trembling truth. Let the memory of sacred tradition wrap around you one last time, if only so you can bless it and release it.

Then… listen.

Not to the voices that tell you you're straying.

Not to the dogma that shames you into silence.

Not to the fear that insists love must come with conditions.

Listen to what *remains* when all of that falls quiet. The still voice within. That gut flutter when truth hits you in a way you can't explain. The ache in your chest when you read a passage and feel like someone finally named what you've carried for years. The way your body softens — not in surrender, but in recognition.

That is truth.

That is your compass.

That is your homecoming.

You do not have to renounce everything you once believed.

You do not have to declare war on the version of you who once found comfort in tradition. You do not have to choose between reverence and liberation.

You are allowed to hold gratitude for what was and still walk toward what is becoming.

You do not need to label yourself. You do not need to prove your worth to any pulpit or priest. You only need to be honest about what no longer fits.

Because your journey is sacred.

Your questions are sacred.

Your expansion is sacred.

Your voice — the one you were told was too much, too curious, too unruly — is sacred.

You were never meant to shrink inside a system that could not hold your truth. If no one else tells you this, I will:

You are not lost. You are being found — by the parts of you that were buried under fear. You are remembering — what it feels like to know and trust your own spirit. You are returning — to a Divine who never needed a title or a steeple to love you.

You are not alone. You are not wrong. You are not broken.

You are becoming.

Your home is not built from borrowed beliefs or dusty rituals.

Your home is made of breath. Of Earth. Of fire. Of wildness. Of wisdom. Of fierce compassion. Of Divine presence that lives not above you — but *within* you.

Keep walking.

Keep listening.

Keep becoming.

You are not leaving something behind.

You are stepping into something truer. And it's okay if it doesn't have a name yet.

It's still holy.

Because *you* are.

Chapter Eleven:
Who I am Now, and How I moved Forward

*"This is not the story of what I lost —
it is the story of what I became,
and the sacred life I am still choosing to build."*

Love After Loss

Let's start where we stopped in chapter 5…
"Mom, I need a dad…"

I didn't begin to date just to find a father for my child. I dated to put my toe in the ocean — to see if I could even handle the idea of companionship again. To test if my heart could stretch, even slightly, toward connection after all it had endured.

It wasn't about rushing into love or filling a void; it was about asking myself, *Can I live again?*

Then came the man who would become our next chapter.

He wasn't flashy. He wasn't the image I had once carried in my head. But he was kind. Caring. Genuine. He made me laugh — deep, unguarded, belly laughs I thought would never escape my lips again. He looked at me with gentleness. His energy allowed me to be me. We had an instant connection, one that didn't feel forced or manufactured.

Most of all, he was willing to step into a story that had already begun long before him. Willing to stand beside me and my child as we sifted through the wreckage of what had been, as we carefully pieced together a new version of life.

Fifteen months after the loss, when we finally packed up and left the house that had been both sanctuary and tomb, it wasn't me and my son walking away from the past. It was all three of us walking toward something new.

Hand in hand. A small, trembling hope awakened alongside the grief.

Here's the truth I didn't know until then: healing doesn't mean forgetting. Moving forward doesn't mean erasing.

It means making room — for love again, for laughter again, for the possibility that life, even after devastation, can surprise you.

That man, appearing almost out of nowhere, became my husband and my children's father.

He stood beside me, held me through the echoes of old grief, given us space to mourn when we needed it, and offered a steady presence when we were ready to smile again.

He became the proof that love after loss is not a replacement — it is a rebirth. It is not about covering up what was lost but about expanding the heart to hold both memory and new beginnings.

It is the sacred weaving together of past and present, of pain and joy, of sorrow and resilience, into something beautifully, imperfectly whole.

Yet…There are still old fears that cling to me.

The fear of loss. The fear of burying another husband. The fear of being left alone, of standing at another graveside, of feeling that deep, aching absence all over again.

The fear of opening up, only to have trust shattered.

As we marry and recite wedding vows, do we ever really stop to think about what is actually being spoken. Do we comprehend the weight of what they truly mean?

When I remarried, I did. That line — til death do us part — took on a whole new meaning. Those five little words. I've lived it. It destroyed me. And now, I have to speak them again. It took me several, several seconds to speak those five words. Fear of this happening again front and center in my mind. The hardest words I'd even said again came out in a stumbling whisper. The weight of them burying me.

To release these fears would mean surrendering control — loosening the tight grip I've held on the illusion that I can somehow shield myself from all future pain. It would mean stepping into love without guarantees, without safety nets, without the false comfort of thinking that if I just brace hard enough, I can stop loss from ever touching me again.

It would mean learning to live alongside vulnerability, to welcome it not as a threat but as the very heartbeat of what makes love real, deep, and alive. Because love without vulnerability is only a performance; it is the willingness to be hurt that makes love true.

The hard truth is this: no amount of guarding can stop life from unfolding.

Loss will still come.

Change will still come.

Grief will knock at my door again one day — yet that doesn't mean I should stop reaching for joy in the meantime.

As we grow older, we know in some part of ourselves that death is inevitable. We watch our parents age, and somewhere in the back of our minds, we prepare for that goodbye.

When we marry, we understand — at least in theory — that one day, one of us will be the one left standing. We imagine it far down the road. We plan a lifetime together, decades of shared dreams, the slow and gentle fading of old age.

What we never prepare for is when death comes early.

When only half the dreams have been lived.

When the bed is still warm, the plans still fresh, the future still stretched out before you.

That is when it is the hardest.

That is when it shatters everything you thought you knew.

That is when the idea of vulnerability becomes terrifying, because you've learned, firsthand, how much there is to lose.

Here's the lesson grief is still teaching me, slowly and painfully: If I let the fear of loss lock me away, I miss not only the pain — I miss the joy, too. I miss the laughter, the connection, the tenderness of a life fully lived.

I refuse to let grief steal that from me.

To love again, with all my heart, is not to deny death — it is to defy it.

It is to say: you may come for me one day, however not today.

Today, I will choose joy. Today, I will choose love. Today, I will choose to open my heart, knowing it may break, but trusting it will also expand.

If I'm not here to embrace life and love with courage, then why am I here?

Reshaping Love

Grief has reshaped my entire understanding of love in ways I never could have imagined.

There's a cliché we hear often — never take tomorrow for granted — but I don't just know those words. I have lived them.

I have traced their shape across the hollow of my chest. I have felt their truth settle into my bones. I know what it means to kiss someone goodbye in the morning, thinking you'll see them again that evening, only to discover that the moment you let go was the last time you would ever touch them.

I know what it's like to carry the weight of a final conversation, a final smile, a final glance over your shoulder — the kind of ordinary moments we always assume will be followed by more.

I remember the last kiss my husband gave me. Standing in our living room in front of the fireplace. A long embrace. And he reached up and gently kissed my forehead. I thought how odd. He never does that. He quietly walked out and left. I believe that unique kiss that day was supposed to be something special. No other kiss would have been remembered. It's a kiss I carry and treasure.

Grief breaks more than your heart.

It rewires it.

It teaches you, painfully and irrevocably, the true nature of love.

Grief has taught me that love is not an idea. It's not a promise of someday. It's not a fantasy you can keep waiting for the perfect conditions to arrive.

Love is something alive — immediate, embodied, fiercely present. It is the warmth of hands intertwined, the sound of shared laughter, the comfort of someone's head resting on your shoulder.

It is the way you pour yourself into the people you cherish, without waiting for the "right" moment or perfect timing.

I have learned to embrace each moment as if it matters — because it does.

I have learned to love with my whole heart, no longer rationing my affection or holding back words of tenderness. There is no later. There is only now.

I have learned to say "I love you" not as a special occasion, but as a way of living. I say it often. I say it without hesitation. I say it even when my voice shakes I am generous with hugs, with touch, with kindness, because I know the preciousness of presence. I know that a handheld in the middle of a hard day can mean more than a hundred promises made for tomorrow.

I understand now, in a way I never did before, that love is amplified — not diminished — when shared with openness, fire, and unapologetic honesty alongside the right person. It's not about guarding your heart or playing it safe.

It's about risking, opening, showing up, even knowing that life is fragile, that nothing is guaranteed.

Because in the end, it's not about the words we said.

It's about the love we showed.

The memories we created.

Those moments when we showed up fully, with open vulnerability.

It's about the pieces of ourselves we gave freely, without hesitation, while we had the chance.

Grief has burned away my hesitation. It has taught me that no one is promised another sunrise. It has taught me that the only thing worse than losing someone is realizing you hold back when you had the chance to love them more fully.

Now, I choose to love—fully, fearlessly.

I love without guarantees.

I love even when I'm afraid — because I know that love, in the end, is the only thing we carry with us, the only thing that lingers after we're gone, the only thing that survives loss, grief, and time.

And perhaps most sacred of all, grief has taught me that love is not something I give to others — it is something I must extend to myself.

To honor the one who grieved. To hold space for the one who survived. To remind the woman I am becoming that she, too, is worthy of tenderness, of care, of being loved not despite her scars, but because of them.

This is the love I know now.

This is the love I live now.

I will never take it for granted again.

Work That Heals

Alongside love, I've discovered work that heals — not just for me, but for others. Losing everything forced me to rebuild, and in that rebuilding, I found a new career, a new calling, a passion I didn't even know lived within me.

I'm not sure how or why it unfolded this way — perhaps it was the guidance of something greater, perhaps it was my own soul pulling me forward — but I found myself enrolling in massage school.

What began as an exploration became a revelation. Healing touch came naturally to me, as if my hands had been waiting their whole life to offer comfort.

I opened a massage practice, yet it was never about technique or muscles — it became a sacred space where I could offer presence, where I could hold the aching, grieving, weary bodies of others and say, through touch: you are not alone.

I know this ache.

I know this longing for comfort.

I am here.

As time passed and my personal journey deepened, I felt another call rising: a spiritual calling, one that invited me to step beyond the familiar and into the unknown.

In the heart of the Bible Belt, where tradition and doctrine run deep, I took a leap of faith and opened a second business — "Beyond Us." This wasn't a storefront or a service list; it was a living, breathing community space.

A place for spiritual advising, psychic reading, chakra balancing, Reiki healing — and perhaps most importantly, a spiritual gathering space where people could come together, month after month, to explore the big, messy, beautiful questions of life.

161

What does it mean to belong?

What does it mean to heal?

What does it mean to connect to the Divine — not through rigid doctrine, but through personal experience?

"Beyond Us" has become a home for seekers, for wanderers, for those craving something beyond the walls of organized religion. And in creating that space, I discovered something profound: the healing I offered to others was also healing me.

Every client, every circle, every conversation became part of my own restoration. I realized that my losses, my grief, my unraveling had made room for something extraordinary — a life of service, a life of meaning, a life where I could stand in my truth and invite others to do the same.

Right beside me, as he always is, stands my husband — immersed in the same passion, walking this path with me.

Together, we have built not just a business, but a sanctuary: a place where we both can pour our hearts into guiding, supporting, and uplifting others.

This is more than work.

This is soul-work.

It is the sacred weaving of pain and purpose, the transformation of past wounds into present light.

Every day, I am profoundly grateful to be here, living it.

Learning to Live Without Answers

Still, some mysteries remain.

The cold case of my husband's death lingers like a shadow at the edge of my life — officially unsolved, unresolved, unanswered.

Over the years, I sought clarity, not only from the sheriff's office, but from voices beyond the earthly systems I had trusted. I reached out to six different psychics, across five different states, none of whom knew each other. Yet each echoed the same haunting message: let it go. They warned that pursuing the investigation further would not bring peace — only danger.

Again and again, on the anniversaries of his death, I found myself standing at the sheriff's office, asking the same aching questions: Is there anything new? Is there anything you can tell me? And again and again, I walked away with nothing but the hollow ache of more questions, the quiet frustration of answers withheld, the gnawing suspicion that there was more beneath the surface I would never fully know.

So, over time, I learned to loosen my grip — not because I stopped caring, but because I realized I could not live shackled to uncertainty.

I learned to hold the mystery, to surrender my need for resolution on this earthly plane.

I learned to live not in the false comfort of certainty, but in a deeper trust — not trust in human institutions, but trust in the quiet, intuitive, spiritual guidance that has shaped so many of my choices.

I believe now that when I cross to the other side, when I stand face to face with the vastness of what lies beyond, I will have my answers. I will know the whole story.

Perhaps, just perhaps, there has been mercy in not knowing right now — perhaps the truth, if laid bare too soon, would break me.

So, I have chosen to walk forward, not in denial, but in surrender.

To let the mystery remain a mystery.

To let the unanswered questions soften, not harden my heart.

To trust that in time — in a time beyond time — I will see the full picture, and it will make sense in a way it cannot here.

In the meantime, I choose to keep living — not weighed down by the unfinished story but lifted by the life I still have. I choose to keep loving, keep trusting, keep building, knowing that my soul's journey is not limited to this one chapter, this one loss, this one set of unanswered questions.

This is the essence of spiritual resilience: not pretending the pain doesn't exist, not forcing closure where there is none, but learning to live in the tension between what I know and what I may never know.

It is the quiet, daily practice of saying — even here, even now — I will walk forward. I will make meaning. I will find peace, not because every question has been answered, but because I have found the strength to hold the mystery with grace.

That, I believe, is where true healing lives.

From Doctrine to Personal Connection

This brings me to the deepest transformation of all: the profound freedom I have found in my evolving spirituality.

I didn't come to spirituality because life was easy or because everything made sense.

I came to it because life cracked me open. Losing my husband, walking through unbearable grief, facing the empty spaces no one else could fill — these weren't experiences that shattered me beyond repair. They were experiences that expanded me, forced me to stretch beyond the limits of what I thought I knew, and made me ask bigger, more soul-stirring questions.

In that aching expansion, I discovered that I do believe there is a power greater than us — someone, someone's, something. A force, an energy, a sacred presence that shaped this world and, in some mysterious way, shaped me.

I no longer believe in the God I was once taught — the God of control, of hierarchy, of rewards and punishments. That God, the one preached from pulpits and written into doctrines, was built on fear, on submission, on the constant, exhausting need to prove worthiness.

The Divine I know now is unlike anything before.

It is not a distant figure sitting on a throne, keeping score. It is not an angry judge waiting to test or punish me. Instead, it is a presence that moves through love, through compassion, through freedom.

I feel it in the natural world — in the hush of the forest, in the rhythm of the ocean, in the warmth of sunlight across my skin.

I sense it in the small, quiet kindnesses of neighbors, in the unexpected generosity of strangers, in the subtle, sacred threads of connection that remind me we are all part of something much larger and more beautiful than we can comprehend.

This Divine presence does not silence my questions — it invites them. It does not shrink me into obedience — it encourages me to grow. It challenges me, not to punish, but to strengthen and stretch my soul. It does not demand blind loyalty or rigid ritual but offers me the grace of choice.

When I am quiet — when I tune out the noise of expectation, fear, and societal conditioning — I can hear its whisper.

That whisper lives in the deepest parts of me, in the "gut knowing," in the sacred intuition we are so often taught to ignore. It speaks in subtle nudges, in the dreams that linger when I wake, in the moments when I pause just long enough to feel held by something unseen.

This is not a connection built from scripture or rules. It is not something handed to me by an institution. It is a living, breathing relationship that walks with me through every moment, in every breath, in every rise and fall of my journey.

I've come to embrace spirituality by letting it be alive — not fixed, not confined to one system or tradition, but growing alongside me, shifting with me, evolving as I evolve.

Some days it shows up as prayer, some days as tears, some days as a simple breath, a candle lit in memory, or a quiet moment of stillness where I remember that I am part of something vast, something loving, something that holds me even when I feel alone.

I've found the Divine — whether you call it God, the Universe, Spirit, Source — not in perfection, but in presence. In the ordinary. In the everyday choice to trust, to soften, to stay open, even after heartbreak, even after betrayal, even after loss.

Today, I stand not as someone who has all the answers, but as someone who has found a home in the questions.

I have found a spiritual belonging not inside church walls, but scattered across the open world, in the spaces where love, intuition, and mystery meet. And here, right here, in this moment, I am at peace.

I am home — not because I have arrived at some perfect destination, but because I have learned to let the Divine walk with me, wherever I am, however I am, holding me always, in every sacred, imperfect step.

How I Hope My Story Can Help Others

I am not here as someone offering perfect answers, tidy resolutions, or polished wisdom. I didn't climb out of grief with a checklist or a spiritual to-do list. I didn't figure it all out.

I survived. I lived it. I stayed with it. And that, in itself, is a kind of wisdom — not the kind that preaches, but the kind that walks in silence beside you and says, *"Me too."*

I offer living proof — proof that you can walk through grief and not disappear. That you can stand at the edge of everything you thought you knew — shattered, disoriented, undone — and still choose to stay. Still choose to breathe. Still choose to take one trembling step at a time toward something that feels like hope.

My story isn't helpful because my healing was flawless. It's helpful because I let it be messy. Because I didn't bypass the hard parts. I didn't tie everything up with a bow or force a silver lining. I sat in the rubble. I wept in the silence. I screamed into the void. I asked questions that had no answers. I kept showing up anyway.

I stayed.

I stayed when the grief made no sense and no one had the words.

I stayed through the unraveling of everything I was taught to believe.

I stayed through the loneliness of finding a path no one else around me understood.

I stayed with the ache, with the doubt, with the spiritual confusion that cracked my foundation in two.

Staying — breathing, trying again, daring to trust even when trust felt dangerous — has become my quiet, powerful testimony.

I've learned that healing is not a straight line. It's not about getting back to who you were before. It's about allowing yourself to become someone new — someone shaped not by pain, but by resilience, by tenderness, by the hard-won wisdom that only comes from walking through fire.

My journey became a reclamation of self. I had to unlearn the belief that being a good woman meant being a quiet one. I had to break the unconscious contracts that told me my pain was a burden, my anger was dangerous, and my truth was too much. I had to learn that grief doesn't make you weak. It makes you honest. Honesty, no matter how raw, is the beginning of all healing.

I gave myself permission to feel what I had spent a lifetime suppressing.

Not just sadness, but rage.

Not just heartbreak, but relief.

Not just fear, but longing. A longing for something real, something sacred, something that didn't require me to pretend or perform. I began to see that grief wasn't a detour from my path. It was the path. The place where my real self finally emerged.

I found a way to connect to the Divine that wasn't filtered through someone else's authority. I stopped begging for signs and started listening for presence. I stopped trying to earn love from a God who felt far away and started noticing the sacred in my own breath, in my own body, in my own becoming.

What I found was not a replacement for religion — it was a return to something older, something wilder, something deep, intimately mine.

If my story can help others, it's not because I have a map — it's because I've walked in the terrain.

I offer not a prescription, but an invitation.

An invitation to trust your own process. To honor your own rhythm. To walk at your own pace, even if that pace is slow, even if it's full of starts and stops, even if you feel like you're still lost.

I want people to know:

You are not broken beyond repair.

You can be loved without shrinking.

You are not behind. You are not late. You are not wrong for where you are.

You can ask questions.

You can rage.

You can rebuild something completely different from what you were given.

You don't have to return to who you were before — because that version of you was never meant to carry the weight of everything you've now lived through. You are becoming.

And that is holy.

You can walk through grief and come out not less, but *more* — more tender, more true, more rooted in your own knowing.

You can let go of what no longer fits — the old roles, the old doctrines, the old metrics of worth — and step into something wildly your own.

You can create your own rituals.

Speak your own prayers.

Build your own relationship with the sacred.

You don't have to do it the way anyone else has.

You only have to do it in a way that feels alive in *you*.

If my story helps in any way, I hope it's because it gives permission — permission to feel everything, to question everything, to lose your way and still find something beautiful.

I hope it shows that grief, though brutal, can become a doorway. That trauma, though devastating, can uncover deep truth. That there is no shame in starting over — in fact, sometimes it's the most spiritual thing we can do.

Because if I can do it — if I can walk through the darkest nights, rebuild from the ashes, find love again, find purpose again, and claim a faith that feels like home — then maybe, just maybe, you can too.

Final Reflection

I stand here now, not as the woman I was before loss, nor as the woman loss tried to shatter — but as someone entirely new. Someone shaped by both heartbreak and healing, by both grief and grace.

My journey is not finished; it never will be.

I have learned that even without all the answers, even with scars and unanswered questions, I am still worthy of love, of joy, of belonging, and of peace.

And so are you.

If you carry anything from these pages, let it be this:

You deserve to rise again.

You deserve to build again.

You deserve to become someone new — not in spite of what you've lost, but because of how deeply you've lived.

Epilogue

There is a moment, after the long storm has passed, when you finally look up and realize you are still here. You've walked through the fire. You've faced the unthinkable. You've sat in the ash and wondered if you would ever rise again.

Then, slowly, without fanfare or warning, you realize: You have risen.

Not as the person you were before — but as someone new. Someone shaped not by survival, but by transformation. Someone who has loved and lost and loved again. Someone who has questioned everything and still chooses to believe — not because they were told to, but because they have found a truth that lives inside their own bones.

I never set out to rebuild my life this way. I never imagined I would carry both a past I cannot change and a future I now shape with intention. I never expected that grief would leave behind gifts — a fiercer voice, a clearer heart, a deeper connection to the Divine.

I know this now: some catalysts arrive gently and shift our course like wind. Others arrive like bombs. My husband's death was the latter — a soul-shattering explosion that reduced everything I knew to rubble.

If not for that moment, I would not be on this path.

I wouldn't be a massage therapist. I wouldn't be a psychic. I wouldn't be doing the spiritual work I do now — helping others speak to their loved ones on the other side, helping them uncover their truth, their path, their purpose. I wouldn't own two businesses. I wouldn't have the loving partnership I now share. I wouldn't be here, holding this book in my hands, telling you that it's possible to begin again.

People don't always understand when I say it's been both a blessing and a curse. But that's the truth. This grief — this violent, sacred catalyst — blew up everything I thought I knew, and in its place, it planted something I couldn't have imagined: a life more honest, more aligned, more deeply connected than anything I had before. Pain cracked me open. But it didn't destroy me. It revealed me.

I never expected to be the person I am today. I totally different person than who I originally was. The quiet one who sat in the background and watched. Holding back from being seen or heard. A shadow, going through the motion, but not truly living.

Here I stand.

I am no longer the woman who walks through life bracing for the next blow. I am the woman who has learned to soften, even knowing how easily things can break. I am the woman who has learned to trust her own intuition, to listen to the whispers of the Divine not from a pulpit or a doctrine, but from the quiet places inside. I am the woman who has learned that healing is not the absence of scars, but the presence of strength.

I want you to know: you can be that person, too. You can walk through your own shadows and come out more whole, not less. You can ask your biggest questions and still find peace in the mystery. You can lose everything you thought mattered — and still, somehow, create a life of beauty, depth, and meaning.

This is not the end of the story. This is not the neat closing of a chapter, the tying of a final bow. This is a pause, a breath, a moment to stand at the edge of all that has been and whisper, I am still here. I am still becoming. And I am ready to keep going.

Wherever you are on your journey, know this:

You are not broken beyond repair.

You are not alone in your questions, your grief, or your longing.

You are being held — by the unseen, by the Divine, by your own resilient spirit that has carried you this far.

Keep walking.

Keep rising.

Keep remembering who you are and who you are still meant to be.

The next chapter is waiting.

You, dear one, are ready.

Acknowledgments

To David – my husband and Warriors Blood, soul companion. You who walked into my life like a breath of fresh air and showed me that love could be safe. You were there not just in laughter, but in the unspoken spaces of healing. You selflessly gave me the space to write this book, remember the husband I once had, and finally heal. For that, I'm forever grateful.

To my children – I have purposely left you out of this book. Your stories are yours to tell – not mine. I give you that love and respect to share if you ever choose to. You have witnessed and endured more than most children ever should. Your presence, your resilience, and your love have been my foundation in life. You are the ones that have anchored me here and kept me going through all the struggles.

To Van and Jan - Where do I even begin? You have walked beside me through every twist of this dark journey. We experience the same lost memories – as the grief was too overwhelming. You witnessed our lives - never questioning, never hesitating. It was you who carried me when I couldn't think, decide, or even breathe. I am forever grateful for all you have done, not just for me, but for our children. You have loved them as your own. You are, in every way that matters as much their parents as I am.

To Peggy, my mentor, guide, and spiritual mother - you were the first to remind me I was never lost, just called. You opened the door and taught me how to listen with the body and not the ears.

To Gabbie, my dearest friend, my inspiration. Without you I would never have written this book. You gave me the inspiration to finally sit down and do it. You fostered the healing I finally deserved.

To my readers - thank you for holding these pages in your hands and allowing my story to echo something in your own. May this book be a mirror, a balm, and a reminder that your truth holds sacred value, too

Religious systems taught me rejection when I needed grace. They turned their back in my moment of greatest need, and that wound is still healing. My anger isn't the absence of faith, it's what remains when you love something enough to grieve how it failed you.

And yet - Spirit never left.

Spirit kept whispering.

Spirit stood by me when the church would not.

For that Presence - wild, nameless, eternal - I offer my deepest thanks.

Coming Soon: A New Chapter in the Soul Journey Trilogy

Spirituality Bloomed from Grief
Pain Became My Teacher – Faith Became My Own
Book Two: The Turning

Grief didn't just break me — it stripped away everything I thought I knew. It also opened something ancient within me.

Where *When God Went Silent* walked through the Shattering, this book emerges from the silence that followed — the space where a whisper, a knowing, a sacred inner voice began to rise. Not from doctrine or dogma, but from within the soft unfolding of my own soul.

This is not a roadmap. It is a remembrance. A holy permission to stop performing your faith — and start reclaiming it.

In these pages, I offer the Turning:

The quiet, relentless shift from what was handed down to what is divinely rising from within. Here, spirituality is no longer inherited. It is something unearthed. Lived. Felt. Reclaimed.

Through personal story, reflection, and soul-deep honesty, *Spirituality Bloomed from Grief* invites you to trust the ache as a portal. To follow your own knowing. To discover a God who was never lost — waiting for you to recognize it within yourself.

If *When God Went Silent* helped you survive the breaking, this next book will help you live through the Becoming.

About the Author

Lea Riley is a spiritual advisor, intuitive guide, and energy healer who came into her calling not through tradition — but through devastation.

When her husband died unexpectedly, the version of God she had grown up with went silent. What followed was not grief, but unraveling — of doctrine, identity, and everything she once believed would keep her safe. In that silence, she didn't find answers. She found truth.

Through body-based wisdom, spiritual curiosity, and the gradual awakening of her intuitive gifts, she rebuilt from the inside out. No longer bound by religious indoctrination, Lea now walks a sacred path rooted in the Divine Feminine, personal sovereignty, and direct communion with Spirit.

Today, she helps others navigate their own seasons of loss, awakening, and soul reclamation. As a psychic medium and energy healer, her work guides others back to the truths their bodies remember — and the Divine that never left.

She is the author of *Awakening the Sacred Self: A Reflective Workbook for Healing, Shadow Work & Soul Integration* (June 2025), and the creator of soul-led tools for transformation, including oracle decks, rituals, and guided spiritual workbooks.

Her work isn't about fixing. It's about remembering — the voice you were taught to silence, the power you were born with, and the sacred within you that was never lost... only waiting.

Walk With Me on Your Sacred Path

If this book stirred something in you — a memory, a question, a quiet yearning — you're not alone.
Awakening isn't a finish line. It's a sacred unfolding.
Sometimes, we need a witness. A companion. A guide.

As a spiritual advisor and psychic, I offer one-on-one sessions by phone or video to support your inner journey. These aren't scripted readings or surface-level insights. These conversations hold sacred meaning — deep, intuitive, and attuned to your soul's unfolding. Whether you're:

- Navigating grief or loss
- Wrestling with spiritual deconstruction
- Feeling called but unsure where to begin
- Awakening gifts you don't yet know how to trust
- Or craving a deeper connection with the Divine...

This space is for you. Together, we'll explore:

- What's stirring within you and why
- How to interpret intuitive nudges and energetic shifts
- Gentle ways to move through shadow work and emotional healing
- Practices for integrating soul wisdom into your everyday life

This work is sacred — rooted in presence, spiritual truth, and deep compassion. You don't have to walk this path alone.

To schedule a session or learn more, visit:
BeyondUsAR.com
Info@BeyondUsAR.com

Let's step into your becoming — together.